THE COLD WAR 1945–1963

Studies in European History

General Editor: Richard Overy
Editorial Consultants: John Breuilly
Roy Porter

THE COLD WAR 1945–1963

M.L. DOCKRILL

First published 1988 by
MACMILLAN PRESS LTD
Houndmills, Basingstoke, Hampshire RG21 6XS
and London
Companies and representatives
throughout the world

ISBN 0-333-40380-0

A catalogue record for this book is available
from the British Library.

This book is printed on paper suitable for recycling and
made from fully managed and sustained forest sources.

12 11 10 9 8 7 6
03 02 01 00 99 98

Printed in Malaysia

Contents

Note on References

References are cited throughout in brackets according to the numbering in the general bibliography, with page references where necessary indicated by a colon after the bibliography number.

Editor's Preface

The main purpose of this new series of Macmillan studies is to make available to teacher and student alike developments in a field of history that has become increasingly specialised with the sheer volume of new research and literature now produced. These studies are designed to present the 'state of the debate' on important themes and episodes in European history since the sixteenth century, presented in a clear and critical way by someone who is closely concerned himself with the debate in question.

The studies are not intended to be read as extended bibliographical essays, though each will contain a detailed guide to further reading which will lead students and the general reader quickly to key publications. Each book carries its own interpretation and conclusions, while locating the discussion firmly in the centre of the current issues as historians see them. It is intended that the series will introduce students to historical approaches which are in some cases very new and which, in the normal course of things, would take many years to filter down into the textbooks and school histories. I hope it will demonstrate some of the excitement historians, like scientists, feel as they work away in the vanguard of their subject.

The format of the series conforms closely with that of the companion volumes of studies in economic and social history which has already established a major reputation since its inception in 1968. Both series have an important contribution to make in publicising what it is that historians are doing and in making history more open and accessible. It is vital for history to communicate if it is to survive.

R.J. OVERY

Map I   Soviet expansion in Europe 1945–8

Legend:
- The 'Iron Curtain' from 1948
- Germany since 1945
- 1937 frontiers
- Allied control zones of Germany and Austria
- Ceded to Russian zone by Britain & America
- Annexed by Russia in 1945
- States which became Communist between 1945 & 1948
- Yugoslav gains from Italy 1945

SOVIET EXPANSION IN EUROPE, 1945-48

Annexed or under Soviet administration			
YEAR	COUNTRIES	POPULATION millions	AREA sq. mls
1940	Part of Finland	0.5	17,600
1940	Estonia	1.1	18,300
1940	Latvia	2.0	25,400
1940	Lithuania	3.0	21,500
1945	Part of German East Prussia	1.2	5,400
1945	Part of Poland	11.8	69,900
1945	Part of Czechoslovakia	0.7	4,900
1945	Part of Rumania	3.7	19,400
	TOTAL:	24.0	182,400

Controlled by U.S.S.R.			
1945	Soviet Zone of Germany	18.8	42,900
1945	Poland	26.5	120,355
1948	Czechoslovakia	12.3	49,381
1947	Hungary	9.8	35,902
1948	Rumania	16.1	91,584
1946	Bulgaria	7.2	42,796
1946	Albania	1.2	10,629
	TOTAL:	91.9	393,547

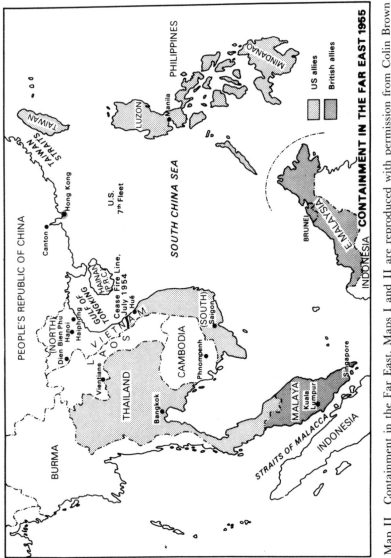

Map II Containment in the Far East. Maps I and II are reproduced with permission from Colin Brown and Peter J. Mooney, *Cold War to Détente 1945–80* (London: Heinemann Educational Books, 1976, 2nd edn 1981) pp. 11, 54.

General Introduction

The Cold War has been defined as a state of extreme tension between the superpowers, stopping short of all-out war but characterised by mutual hostility and involvement in covert warfare and war by proxy as a means of upholding the interests of one against the other. The Cold War remained 'cold' because the development of nuclear weapons had made resort to war a suicidal enterprise: both sides would be totally devastated by such an eventuality. The struggle between the two sides has accordingly been carried out by indirect means, very often at considerable risk, and the resulting tensions have ensured that both sides have maintained a high and continuous state of readiness for war. The massive expenditures by both sides on research and development of nuclear arsenals and delivery vehicles has led to a spiralling arms race which could, in turn, as a result of miscalculation by one side or the other, have led to a holocaust. There is a huge bibliography seeking to interpret and explain the origins and development of the 'Cold War'. Inevitably these interpretations have changed in response to the influence of contemporary developments on the writers. For the most part the writings of Western historians in the late 1940s and 1950s have reflected the preoccupation of the governing elite with the evils of communism. United States diplomats had experienced the menacing nature of the Soviet state at first hand during the 1930s and many of them had not been converted to a more favourable view during the high summer of Soviet-American friendship during the Second World War. Their warnings about Soviet malevolence in 1945 and 1946 coincided with the discovery by top American decision-makers in Washington that co-operation with the Soviet Union was likely to prove more difficult than they had

1

anticipated during that war. Memories of wartime obstructionism by Soviet bureaucrats and of their scant gratitude for American aid were rekindled after 1945 as the Soviets tenaciously clung to their notions of post-war security – notions which clashed with American expectations of continuing collaboration [25].

As the world plunged into the Cold War, American historians took up the theme of the fundamental antagonism of the communists for the capitalist system and, in the process, exaggerated the Soviet threat to the West, instensifying the apprehensions of a generation of American students and thus helping to fuel the anti-communist hysteria which gripped the United States in the early 1950s. The appeals for restraint by cooler heads, such as George Kennan, were ignored. United States policy-makers and academics were deluged with a flood of information about Soviet intentions, all of which seemed to confirm their existing view of the sinister and dangerous nature of Soviet policy. In the same way, Soviet writers, most of whom were long schooled in the Leninist view that the capitalist system was fundamentally hostile to socialism, would have been unwise to voice contrary opinions while Stalin was closing off the Soviet Union from Western influences and consolidating his hold on the border states, especially as, in any case, American policy seemed to confirm their prejudices.

When Cold War tensions began to subside later, American historians turned against the prevailing orthodoxy. During the late 1960s and early 1970s Western interpretations of the Cold War were affected by the costly and seemingly endless conflict in Vietnam. A revisionist school of historians emerged, chiefly American, who tended to blame the United States for originating the Cold War and for extending it. Stalin was now seen as essentially a cautious and defensive leader, with the United States misinterpreting and over-reacting to his efforts to protect Soviet security, thus making a tense situation even more dangerous. These writers argued that the rift between the two superpowers was the result of the ambitions of a United States which had grown rich and powerful during the Second World War and which, after 1945, wanted to extend her power throughout the world by

2

the exercise of her immense financial strength. In order to achieve this ambition she sought overseas markets and investment opportunities. This capitalist imperative clashed with the insistence of the Soviet Union on preserving her particular socio-economic system, much weakened by the destruction inflicted on her during the Second World War. Thus the Soviet Union's policy towards the United States was dictated by the necessity of avoiding being overwhelmed by American capitalism, which would have turned the Soviet Union into a mere raw materials base for the West. The Cold War arose when the United States attempted to exercise her economic strength in Central and Eastern Europe, an area whose control by the Soviet Union was vital to Soviet security [29; 40; 61].

During the later 1970s, with the opening of United States archives to academic scrutiny, under the Freedom of Information Act, a new school of so-called post-Vietnam revisionists emerged. John Lewis Gaddis is a leading exponent of this school. It resulted in a more sophisticated analysis of the origins of the Cold War, which sought to demonstrate that the clash between the United States and the Soviet Union arose from misunderstandings of each other's policies and was often the result of over-reaction by both sides to often defensive moves by the other [24]. Other American writers have investigated more carefully available material on Soviet policy in these years – the input from Soviet historians has usually been both inadequate and affected by ideological considerations. These American 'Sovietologists' have demonstrated what was obvious to Western diplomats in Moscow at the time – that Stalin alone could never have controlled the Soviet Union completely after 1945. The complex society which Russia had become after the Second World War could not have been ruled single-handedly by one man [48]. Whole areas of internal policy were controlled by the bureaucracy with little, if any, reference to the Politburo. Nevertheless these writers admit that Stalin managed to keep a close watch on foreign policy decisions while his associates remained intimidated by him, and he was still capable of exerting his authority in matters of crucial importance to the Soviet Union. Even at the end of his life

3

it is clear that he was meditating a purge of the other communist leaders. Thus, while these historians have drawn our attention to the difficulty of regarding the Soviet Union as a pure dictatorship in those years, it is still evident that Stalin, despite the struggles in which he had to engage, succeeded in maintaining his overall power in the Soviet Union, even if there were frequent fluctuations in foreign policy as a result [58].

In the same way Khrushchev's internal difficulties and his struggle with his political and military adversaries in the Soviet Union are now seen as more crucial to the changes of policy towards the West in the 1950s and early 1960s – a combination of bluster and threats mingled with appeals for peaceful co-existence – than Khrushchev's own mercurial temperament, although this must have had some effect [43].

Thus the Cold War in recent historiography has been seen as a product of miscalculation rather than malevolence by both sides. However, in the last analysis Western writers still see the Soviet Union as the prime motivator: her suspicions and mistrust of the West condemned the world to a bi-polar struggle for power while the United States was criticised for over-reacting to Soviet actions.

Norman Graebner, a leading historian of the Cold War, has suggested that deeper causes than misunderstandings between the United States and the Soviet Union were responsible for the Cold War, and these lay deep within American history and tradition. Developments since 1945 can be ascribed, he believes, to the marriage of American idealistic universalism – that American values of liberty and constitutionalism have worldwide applicability – to the new-found military and material might of the United States. Before 1941 the United States did not have the power to project her ideology beyond the shores of the continent (except in Latin America, which the United States had long claimed as her special sphere of interest). Thus her efforts to apply the doctrine of 'The Open Door' to trade and investment in China before 1914 were a conspicuous failure there. The United States did not have the military force or the desire to impose her ideals on that country, whereas Russia, Japan and Britain were able and willing to carve

China up economically into spheres of interest. In 1918 and 1919 Woodrow Wilson secured the reluctant approval of the other victor powers to the application to the peace treaties of his own particular brand of messianic liberalism, national self-determination and a League of self-governing nations, but these were repudiated by his own people.

After 1947 the United States possessed the power and the will to try to impose her ideals on other peoples. As Graebner points out, this kind of universalism, as expressed in the Truman and Eisenhower Doctrines, was often not only repugnant to its intended beneficiaries who, with some justice, suspected that it was a cover behind which the United States was pursuing her own interests, but that even a powerful nation like the United States was, in the last resort, incapable of imposing her will on them, as the Vietnam War demonstrated so starkly. The result, as after 1919, was frustration and disillusionment, and a retreat from universalism. However, a recovery of American self-confidence in the 1980s led to a new surge of 'Pax Americana'.

The so-called *realpolitik* school of historians of the Cold War – Graebner, Louis Hallé and Hans J. Morgenthau, although the latter is more a theorist of international relations than a historian – has either downgraded or dismissed altogether the importance of ideology as a factor in American and Soviet foreign policy. They consider ideology a mask behind which the two superpowers pursue their own selfish interests and a means of justifying their policies to the outside world. Thus these writers see little difference between the diplomatic manoeuvres of the nineteenth-century European states – German Chancellor Otto von Bismarck is seen as the most skilful practitioner – and the activities of the twentieth-century superpowers. They see ideology as merely an additional weapon in the diplomatic arsenal, a propaganda tool to rally their own people behind them, to undermine the will of the adversary's population and to appeal to the uncommitted elsewhere.

While there is some truth in this assumption, it is not of course the whole truth. Marxism-Leninism is the basic tenet of the Soviet state. It is regarded as the cornerstone of the organisation of the Soviet Union and its teachings provide the goal towards which communists should strive. However cynical men like Malenkov and Khrushchev may have been in other respects, communism motivated them and they genuinely believed that its so-called blessings had universal application. In the same way the liberal Christian and capitalist ideology of the United States is wholeheartedly accepted by most Americans, and reinforces their patriotism and love of country. It was an inspiration to men like Truman, Eisenhower and Kennedy who also believed in the universality of its appeal.

During the 1950s and 1960s the United States devoted considerable energies to promoting her anti-communist missionary zeal and in the process world tension was increased rather than diminished. Dulles's frequent diatribes against the so-called world communist conspiracy suggested that no compromise was possible with the forces of evil. Later his bellicose language was matched by Khrushchev's own brand of sabre-rattling. While Eisenhower was slightly more flexible and was prepared to make a few harmless gestures of amiability towards Moscow, he also believed that a true meeting of minds between the United States and the Soviet Union was impossible while the Soviet regime survived in its existing form. In any case this indifference reflected the assumption that the United States was strong enough to act as the world's policeman and had no need of arms agreements or closer relations with the Soviet Union, even if these had been on offer.

John F. Kennedy was uniquely qualified to continue and extend Eisenhower's anti-communist crusade. Relatively young, arrogant and forceful, he claimed that his idealism was more sincere, purposeful and progressive than that of his complacent predecessor. In his speeches he extolled the American dream of liberty and prosperity as a universal goal. Critics continued to point out that the consequences seemed to be that the United States supported regimes like those of Rhee in South Korea and (until 1963) of Diem in South Vietnam, whose ideas about liberty and freedom were not founded in any way upon American precepts.

The Cuban missile crisis had the effect of increasing the already bounding confidence of the United States in her own destiny. President Johnson's decision to commit American air and ground forces to South Vietnam in 1965 reflected this vision of an all-powerful United States actively combating the spread of communism and defending American values in the free world. The reality, of course, was more complicated and the arguments suspect. When the Vietnam intervention failed to achieve its purpose, President Nixon reduced the American commitment there and finally abandoned South Vietnam altogether. He turned instead to the normalisation of American relations with Communist China and to *détente* with the Soviet Union. Ideological considerations did not take long to resurface. The election of Ronald Reagan to the presidency in 1980 was based partly on the suspicion that the Soviet Union had taken advantage of the temporary weakness of the United States after Vietnam to expand her armaments and extend her power and influence in the Third World. Reaganism represented a renewed American determination to counter and overturn this communist challenge.

1 From the First World War to the Cold War, 1919–1946*

(i) 1917–1941

Antagonism had been inherent in the American-Soviet relationship since the Bolshevik Revolution of 1917. The two great continental states represented totally opposed ideologies: the United States the values of liberal, capitalist democracy, while the Soviet Union was the first 'socialist republic', a communist dictatorship dedicated to spreading 'world revolution' by overthrowing the existing world order. These ideological differences were starkly revealed as the First World War ended in November 1918 and a peace conference, at which Russia was not represented, convened in Paris in January 1919. United States war aims, as expressed in Woodrow Wilson's Fourteen Points speech of the previous year, envisaged a world based on the principle of national self-determination and a League of Nations which would replace the unstable pre-1914 system of alliances and balance of power politics. The Soviets, on the other hand, led by V.I. Lenin, insisted that the worldwide victory of the proletariat was the only basis for a peaceful world. Western assistance to anti-communist forces in Russia attempting to overthrow the Bolshevik regime in the early post-war years heightened the suspicions of the Soviet leadership about the implacable hostility of the capitalist states towards them, and about their determination to crush the new Soviet republic. Woodrow Wilson's vision of a world dedicated to the preservation of peace, in which the United States would

* I am grateful to my colleagues Lawrence Freedman and Brian Holden Reid in the War Studies Department, for reading the manuscript and for their helpful advice, and to Richard Overy of the History Department at King's College, London.

play a major part, was destroyed when the United States Senate in 1920 repudiated the Treaty of Versailles with Germany, which the major allies had negotiated so laboriously in Paris in 1919. The League of Nations Covenant was an integral part of the Treaty and the Senate decision meant that the United States would not be involved in the organisation. Thereafter the United States retreated into isolationism. However, the mutual suspicion between the United States and the Soviet Union did not subside. The United States, angered by the Bolsheviks' repudiation of the Czarist debts owed to the West, refused to recognise the Moscow regime, even after it became clear in 1920 that the Soviet Union would survive both internal and external threats to its existence.

Following the death of V.I. Lenin in 1924, a struggle for power between his heirs led to the emergence of Joseph V. Stalin as Soviet leader. Stalin was less interested than his rivals in exporting revolution and more concerned to build up the Soviet Union's industrial and military base in order that Russia might become the bastion of communism and, as such, able to resist aggression by the capitalist West. The gigantic sacrifices the industrialisation process imposed on the Soviet people and economy led to a preoccupation with internal affairs, just as the onset of the depression in the United States in 1929 had a similar effect in increasing isolationist sentiment there. However, Japanese aggression in Manchuria and China after 1931 prompted Stalin and the newly elected United States President, Franklin Delano Roosevelt, each increasingly concerned about the threat of a militarist Japan to their interests in Asia, to open diplomatic relations with each other in 1933. Stalin agreed to recognise the former Czarist debts in return for a loan from the United States, but this agreement soon foundered on mutual disagreements about its terms. There was little meeting of minds, given their two different systems of government.

On paper the Soviet constitution which Stalin introduced in 1936 guaranteed the Soviet citizens' legal and democratic rights: in practice the Communist Party was supreme, with its powers vested in the party organs of the Politburo and the Secretariat, over which Stalin presided. The Party

9

Congress met seldom, while the All Union Central Committee was a mere rubber stamp for decisions already reached. After Stalin's purges of his former colleagues and of the Red Army in the late 1930s, Stalin's will was unchallenged. These purges disgusted Soviet experts in the State Department and US diplomats in Moscow, such as George F. Kennan: men who were to emerge in senior positions in the State Department and the American diplomatic service during and after the Second World War with their suspicions of the Soviet Union undiminished. They were to exercise an important influence on American foreign policy during the early stages of the Cold War. American hostility towards the Soviet Union during the late 1930s was increased by the signature of the Non-Aggression Pact between the Soviet Union and Nazi Germany in August 1939. This pact resulted in the division of Poland between the two countries after Germany had crushed Polish resistance in September 1939. Soviet neutrality also enabled the German army to defeat France in the spring of 1940 without Germany being distracted by the threat of a Soviet attack in the East. Stalin justified his alliance with Nazi Germany by pointing to the reluctance of Great Britain and France to join the Soviet Union in the 1930s in standing up to Hitler, preferring instead to appease Hitler, with the object, Stalin claimed, of encouraging Germany to turn on Russia. The Soviet Union would therefore remain neutral in this new 'capitalist war'.

Between 1939 and 1941 the Soviet Union supplied Germany with much-needed raw materials. Her treaty with Germany enabled the Soviet Union to secure not only Eastern Poland but also the Baltic Republics, part of Finland, Bessarabia and Northern Bukovina. Stalin later claimed that these acquisitions were intended to provide the Soviet Union with a defensive perimeter should Nazi Germany later become an enemy. However, progress in building these new defences was slow and the task had not been completed by the summer of 1941.

American hostility towards the Soviet Union after 1919 was mild compared with the intensity of the fear and suspicion with which that country was regarded by Britain and France, particularly during the 1920s. These two democracies had taken the lead in organising Western assistance to the anti-communist ('White') forces during the civil war in Russia, when token forces of Anglo-French troops had been despatched to North Russia and the Crimea to fight alongside the Whites. Antagonism in the West towards the Bolsheviks had been provoked by Lenin's decision to withdraw Russia from the war with Germany and to sign a peace treaty with the Central Powers in the spring of 1918. The repudiation by the Bolsheviks of the debts owed to foreigners by the Czarist regime had particularly hurt the French, who had invested large sums in Russia's industrialisation and rearmament programmes before 1914.

After 1918 London and Paris hoped that the Bolsheviks would be destroyed by their internal enemies and in the meantime refused to recognise the regime or allow it (or indeed any of the other contenders for power) to represent Russia at the Paris Peace Conference. Bolshevik propaganda and financial assistance were used to incite revolution amongst the working classes of Western Europe and this caused the ruling classes in the West considerable concern and anger [60]. Subsequent Soviet efforts to spread disaffection in India against British imperialism also made the establishment of stable relations between the Soviet Union and Britain extremely difficult, and indeed, towards the end of the 1920s, British military strategists were drawing up plans for a possible war with Soviet Russia on the north-west frontier of India.

Although the rise of Hitler's Germany after 1933 brought France and Soviet Russia together in a shaky alliance in 1935, the connection remained unpopular in France, and she refused to sign a military convention with her new ally. When the Soviet Union joined the League of Nations and began to call for collective action by the democratic states against fascism, many policy-makers in Western Europe mistrusted her motives, suspecting that this was a new Soviet ruse to project her influence and ideology into Europe. Britain distanced herself from these Soviet appeals for co-operation, preferring to seek agreement with Nazi Germany to preserve peace in Europe and only when this effort failed in 1939 did she join with France in attempting to negotiate a military convention with the Soviet Union. The failure of these talks, followed by the signature of the Nazi-Soviet pact in August 1939, convinced British leaders that their caution had been justified. The Soviet Union's seizure of part of Poland in October 1939, and later of the Baltic States and other border territories in the Balkans, and especially her attack upon Finland in the winter of 1939, were further serious blows to what little remaining credibility the Soviet Union possessed in London and Paris. Indeed, during the Soviet-Finnish war, there was talk in official circles of Anglo-French intervention to assist the Finns against the Soviets.

Thus, despite the dramatic events in the summer of 1941, with the Soviet Union now fighting Germany, a considerable fund of distrust of Soviet ambitions had been built up, particularly in London, during the inter-war period, and this was to resurface after 1945. Indeed, Winston Churchill, British Prime Minister from May 1940 to July 1945, had been the prime mover in organising Western invervention against the Bolsheviks in 1919, and in 1945 he repeatedly urged on an unresponsive Roosevelt and a wavering Truman a more vigorous Western reaction to Soviet challenges in Eastern Europe.

(ii) Soviet-American relations during the Second World War, 1941–1945

When the Germans turned on their former ally and invaded the Soviet Union on 22 June 1941, Winston Churchill and Roosevelt insisted that Britain and the United States should supply the Soviet Union with munitions although their respective military chiefs did not think that the Red Army would survive for more than a few weeks. The two Western leaders were convinced that, unless the Soviet Union received as much material support as their two countries could provide, she was certain to succumb to the German armies. British weakness precluded her from launching even a token attack on German-occupied France to relieve the sorely pressed Russians and divert German troops from the East. It was essential therefore that the West should supply the

Soviet Union with guns, armoured vehicles, aeroplanes and sophisticated military equipment of all kinds of which the Red Army was in critical need. If the Soviet Union collapsed, Nazi Germany would be able to devote all her efforts to subduing Britain and then, backed by captured Soviet raw materials and other resources, she would become a major threat to American security.

By September 1941 both Britain and the Soviet Union were receiving as much material support as the steadily reviving American industrial economy could supply, but the United States remained outside the conflict. While isolationism in the United States was slackening, Roosevelt realised that the American people were opposed to American involvement in another war. The Japanese attack on Pearl Harbor on 7 December 1941, followed by Hitler's declaration of war on the United States, finally brought the latter into the war as an ally of Britain and the Soviet Union against Germany. However, underlying tensions between these three great powers, while hidden from public view, did not diminish. The Soviet Union complained bitterly about the repeated Anglo-American delays in launching a second front – a cross-Channel invasion of France from Britain to relieve German pressure on the Soviet Union. Although there were important logistical and technical arguments against an early cross-Channel invasion, an associated factor in the minds of both Churchill and Roosevelt was the need to avoid heavy losses of American and British lives in a premature assault on German-occupied France. Stalin suspected that the two Western powers intended to let the Soviet Union suffer most of the human and material losses in the war against Germany, and he did not regard the Anglo-American invasions of North Africa and Southern Italy in 1942 and 1943 as substitutes for a full-scale Allied attack into the heartland of the Reich. For their part London and Washington feared that a beleaguered Stalin might make a separate peace with Germany.

By early 1942, when it became clear that, despite her immense losses, the Soviet Union would survive the German onslaught, Stalin exploited these Western fears of a German-Soviet separate peace by demanding Allied recognition of the territorial gains he had made as a result of the Nazi-Soviet pact. In 1944, as his victorious armies began to sweep across Central and Eastern Europe, he pressed the Western powers to agree that the post-war governments of these countries should be pro-Soviet in orientation. Inevitably, since the area would be under Red Army occupation, communist parties would play a leading role in whatever governments were established. Stalin was determined that the region should never again become a conduit for German aggression against the Soviet Union [47].

Stalin's aims did not fit comfortably into Anglo-American notions about the post-war world. By 1944 the United States, having far outstripped Britain in military, economic and industrial strength, was the dominant partner in the alliance, and she fully intended to have a major voice in the post-war settlement. Roosevelt had not formulated a precisely defined post-war peace programme but had instead articulated a set of idealistic principles which were intended to unite both American and Allied opinion against fascism [14]. Although in 1941 Churchill and Stalin had associated themselves with Roosevelt's concept of a post-war world based on the rights of all peoples to self-determination, Stalin had no intention of letting such ideals affect his policy towards Eastern Europe, while Churchill had equally no intention of applying them to the British empire.

Another strand in American thinking about the post-war period, and one which appealed particularly to the American Secretary of State, Cordell Hull, was that the post-war world economic order should be based on the principle of the open door to trade and investment. In Hull's view the rise of the aggressors in Asia and Europe had been primarily the result of the dislocation of the world economy after 1929, when tariff barriers had so diminished world trade that the most economically deprived, and yet vigorous, states like Germany and Japan had turned to overseas expansion for their economic salvation. Thus a renewed post-war slump could be avoided if all nations had equal access to world markets, supplies of raw materials and investment opportunities. As a result world trade would burgeon and all nations, rich and poor, would prosper, thus reducing the economic discontent

14

and the gross inequalities which had provided fertile soil for fascism.

Revisionist American historians, in attempting to counter American accusations that the aggressive behaviour of the Soviet Union had been responsible for the Cold War, used the economic aspects of American planning for the post-war world as a means of laying the major part of the blame on the United States. As two writers of this school put it, 'essentially the United States' aim was to reconstitute the world so that American business could trade, operate and profit without restriction everywhere' [40:6]. They argue that the United States search for world economic domination after the war led to a collision with the Soviet Union, determined not to allow her war-weakened economy to be dominated by American big business. Thus, in this view, the ensuing deterioration in American-Soviet relations resulted from Soviet efforts to defend herself and her interests against American economic expansionism [40:61].

It is true that American economists feared that the United States would face the same problems of reconversion to a peace economy as in 1919, and a world which was open to American exports would lessen the chance that its transition from war to peace would lead to heavy unemployment in the United States. But the revisionist theorists do not satisfactorily explain why increasingly tense Soviet-American relations after 1945 originated in Eastern Europe, an area which had attracted little American trade and investment before 1939 and was not likely to provide the United States with any greater opportunities after 1945 [54]. The revisionists also tend to dismiss as hyprocrisy the very real vein of idealism which animated American conceptions of the post-war world, conceptions which were influenced as much by political as by economic considerations. There is little doubt that the United States did want to see a world reconstructed in her own image after the war, but this did not necessarily suggest the cynical motives the revisionists believe lay behind it. Roosevelt, a shrewd and pragmatic politician, recognised that American ideas about the post-war world would not necessarily be acceptable to the Soviet Union. They did not always appeal to the United States'

15

closest ally, Great Britain. For instance, Churchill rejected Roosevelt's pressure for the decolonisation of the European empires in Asia after the war. Roosevelt feared that the differences between the expectations of his allies and those of American public opinion about the shape of the post-war world might become insurmountable. After the upsurge of internationalism which took place in the United States from 1941 onwards, selfish actions by his allies might lead to corresponding American disillusionment and a revival of the isolationism which, in Roosevelt's view, had done so much to encourage fascist aggression in the 1930s. Indeed, Roosevelt was so concerned to avoid the fate of Woodrow Wilson that he had discouraged talk of a new League after the war, but had emphasised instead a concept of 'Four Policemen' – China, the United States, the Soviet Union and Britain – who would together maintain world peace. When it became clear that the American people wanted something more principled than a world dominated by the big four, Roosevelt had embraced the concept of a United Nations as a peace-keeping organisation. This would consist of a General Assembly of all non-fascist states, but the four-policemen concept would be retained in the Security Council of the great powers, who would exercise effective control of the organisation [14; 16].

Roosevelt attributed much of the American disillusionment with the post-1919 world to the immense gulf between Woodrow Wilson's vision of a just and stable world order and the selfish war aims of the victorious West European powers. In particular the various secret territorial agreements the European allies had concluded with each other during the war, based on spheres of interest and the division of the spoils, clashed with Wilson's hopes for territorial and governmental arrangements based on the will of the peoples involved. This dichotomy contributed to American alienation from the peace settlements. Roosevelt was determined that the United States should not become involved in similar deals during this war and he tried to discourage Britain and the Soviet Union from entering into them. Roosevelt was, however, well aware of the Soviet Union's preoccupation with her security and of the reservations which Moscow and

London entertained towards his principles.

He was not so concerned about Britain's opposition – her economic and financial plight resulting from her wartime sacrifices would make her dependent on the United States after the war. Roosevelt was convinced that post-war peace and stability hinged upon continued Soviet-American co-operation. His main argument was that Nazi Germany had brought the two countries together in uneasy alliance and, once this threat had been removed, there would be little to keep them united. Roosevelt was therefore determined to make the effort, chiefly by means of personal contacts with Stalin designed to convince the Soviet Union that the two powers could co-operate after the war. During his two wartime meetings with the Soviet leader at Teheran in 1943 and Yalta in 1945 he voiced his distrust of Britain and her imperialism to demonstrate to Stalin that there was no Anglo-American bloc ranged against the Soviet Union. At Teheran he hinted to Stalin that the United States would not oppose Poland's post-war frontiers being shifted westward to give the Soviet Union Eastern Poland, with Poland securing as compensation the Oder-Neisse line at the expense of Germany. He also agreed that the Polish government should be reconstituted to exclude anti-Soviet elements. In return for these concessions he urged the Soviet leader to exercise discretion in handling the Poles so as not to antagonise Polish-American voters in the United States. While these undertakings were purely verbal, Stalin undoubtedly believed that he had been given a free hand in Eastern Europe. Conversely, Roosevelt was fully aware that once the Red Army had overrun Eastern Europe, the West would be in no position to influence Soviet behaviour, but he could hardly explain this to the American people. Hence, when Soviet actions in Eastern Europe made a mockery of the principle of self-determination, United States opinion turned against its former ally [24].

Churchill urged Roosevelt to agree to Anglo-American negotiations with Stalin to reach agreement on the limits to Soviet behaviour in Eastern Europe while the Soviet Union was still dependent on the West for assistance. Roosevelt, however, rejected such an Anglo-American front. Negotiations

17

about territorial acquisitions and spheres of influence would lead to dissension between the Allies while the war was still to be won, and would cause an outcry in the United States if they became public knowledge. That was a major reason why Roosevelt did not welcome the so-called 'percentages' agreement which Churchill worked out with Stalin in Moscow in October 1944, giving the Soviets effective control over Romania, Bulgaria and Hungary, joint influence with Britain in Yugoslavia and Britain freedom of action in Greece. In the early post-war years Stalin adhered to this agreement.

Roosevelt thus sought to defer detailed discussion of territorial and other questions until the war was over, since the United Nations would, he believed, provide a forum for the reconciliation of differences between the great powers. Unlike the post-1919 League of Nations, dominated by Britain and France, the United Nations would be a truly worldwide organisation, with the United States, the Soviet Union, Britain and China as founder members. Roosevelt's efforts to remain on good terms with the Soviet Union were assisted by Stalin's relaxation of strict party controls on Soviet culture after June 1941, by his emphasis on the traditional military and patriotic values of Russia and by his toleration of a limited religious revival. American commentators persuaded themselves that these concessions heralded moves towards a more liberal and humane Russian society. Furthermore, the abolition in 1943 of the Communist International – the 'Comintern', an organisation of communist parties set up in March 1919, allegedly independent of Moscow and dedicated to spreading the communist message – signified to many Western observers that the Soviet Union was no longer interested in promoting international communism. Stalin's gestures were intended to stimulate Russian patriotic enthusiasm during a period of acute national emergency, and were not to lead to any far-reaching reforms of the Soviet system. Indeed, the abolition of the Comintern had less to do with its effects on Western opinion and more to do with Stalin's desire to rein in the enthusiasm of European communist parties (who believed that the defeat of Germany and Italy would open the way to revolution in Europe) and bring them firmly under Moscow's control.

18

Stalin had no wish to quarrel with the United States after the war and he was anxious to prevent communist coups in liberated countries which would alienate Western opinion [24; 47].

(iii) The Yalta Conference

On the brink of Germany's defeat, Churchill, Stalin and Roosevelt met for a second time at Yalta in the Crimea between 4 and 11 February 1945 to discuss the future of Europe. Roosevelt refused Churchill's request for a co-ordinated Anglo-American policy at the conference. Roosevelt persisted in his belief that personal discussion with Stalin would be more successful than if the Soviet leader were faced with an Anglo-American effort to 'gang up' against the Soviet Union.

As at Teheran, Roosevelt failed to make clear to Stalin how far he could pursue Soviet aims in Eastern Europe, and the vague wording of the agreements reached at Yalta on the future of the region again left Stalin with the impression that he was being given virtually a free hand. A casual remark by Roosevelt that he doubted that the American people would allow American troops to remain in occupation of Germany for more than two years after the war, and the obvious lack of any carefully thought out American proposal for the future of Germany, may have convinced Stalin that the United States was not greatly concerned about the fate of Central and Eastern Europe. The three powers merely accepted the agreements their officials had reached in 1944 on the military zones the three Allies would occupy in Germany after her surrender – although, on Churchill's insistence, France was also given a small zone. A four-power military council for Germany was set up in Berlin, which was also to be divided into four Allied military sectors. The future of Germany was left for determination by a future peace conference.

This division of Germany was not intended to be permanent. The powers agreed that Germany should be treated as an economic unit. The only post-war plan the Americans had formulated for the country was one drawn up in October 1944 by Henry Morgenthau, the Secretary of the Treasury, which proposed that Germany should be de-industrialised and turned into a pastoral community. Roosevelt and Churchill had assented to this plan at a time when anti-German feelings were running high but, by February 1945, they had come to the conclusion that it was impractical. Neither did Stalin appear to have any definite policy about Germany, except to insist that the Russians should extract as much compensation as possible from the German economy for the damage the Nazis had inflicted on the Soviet Union. At Yalta the Soviets put forward figures of from $10 to $20 billion and demanded that the Soviet Union should receive priority in allocations of German capital equipment and payments in kind for a period of ten years. Since France and other countries occupied by Germany also put forward large reparation claims, this question was likely to cause considerable dissension. Neither the United States nor Great Britain were prepared to permit the Soviet Union and other claimants to seize Germany's resources, thus impairing her chances of future recovery, while they were forced, in order to keep the German people alive, to subsidise Germany's food and raw materials requirements. The conference postponed a decision on this issue by setting up a Reparation Commission to determine how much Germany should pay and in what form she should pay it – although the Soviet claim was accepted as the basis for discussion.

Stalin agreed that the Soviet Foreign Minister, V.M. Molotov, would attend a conference of the victorious powers at San Francisco in April 1945 to set up the United Nations Organisation. He insisted that each of the great powers represented on the executive organ of the United Nations, the Security Council, should have the right to veto any substantive resolution. Having ensured that the United Nations would not be able to thwart future Soviet policy, Stalin was quite willing to support the establishment of the United Nations, in which Roosevelt put so much faith, especially as, in return for Stalin's support, Roosevelt appeared to look sympathetically at Soviet demands else-where.

The three powers also reached a compromise over Poland. Shortly before the Yalta meeting Stalin had recognised a Soviet-backed Polish Communist Committee based at Lublin in Soviet-occupied Poland as the provisional government of Poland. Britain and the United States continued to recognise the Polish government-in-exile in London as the legitimate government, but this had shown itself too anti-Soviet and pro-Western for Stalin's taste. However, the two Western leaders avoided a confrontation over this issue by agreeing that the Lublin Committee was to form the nucleus of a Polish provisional government, with a few members of the London government allotted ministerial posts in this administration. Stalin also promised that free elections would be held in Poland after the war. Finally Stalin proposed that the Soviet Union annex Eastern Poland (with the addition of the former East Prussian port of Königsberg), while Poland was to receive compensation for this at the expense of Germany as far west as the Oder-Western Neisse rivers. Roosevelt, who had hinted at Teheran that he might approve such an arrangement, refused to agree publicly at Yalta to such an obvious breach of the principle of national self-determination. Churchill was even more distressed since, after all, Britain had gone to war in 1939 to defend Poland's integrity but in practice there was little the Western leaders could do to prevent these changes since the Red Army was already in occupation of Eastern Poland, while the Poles were soon to seize the German territories allocated to them, expelling the German population as they did so.

Roosevelt was unwilling to risk a breach with Stalin over Poland, a country in which in any case he appeared to take little interest. On the other hand he was anxious to secure a Soviet promise to enter the war against Japan as soon as possible, as American military experts calculated that without Soviet assistance it would take as much as a further year of bloody struggle to subdue Japanese resistance. Soviet intervention would save many American lives and Roosevelt was greatly relieved when Stalin agreed to declare war on Japan six weeks after the end of the European conflict. However, in return he demanded that the Soviet Union acquire the Japanese Kurile Islands, the southern half of

Sakhalin Island, and railway, economic and port concessions in Chinese Manchuria. Roosevelt agreed to these transfers despite their apparent contradiction of Allied wartime pledges of no territorial aggrandisement.

Finally Stalin decided to sign a three-power Declaration on Liberated Europe which promised that Germany's former allies would be helped 'to solve by democratic means their pressing political and economic problems' and acknowledged 'the right of all peoples to choose the governments under which they lived'. This formula enabled Roosevelt to inform Congress that Yalta had confirmed the Atlantic Charter principles and gave the impression that Stalin was committed to working closely with the West. He did not, however, inform Congress of his agreement to the USSR's gains in the Far East, which led to much criticism when it was revealed later in the year: Roosevelt had also kept it secret from his closest advisers [19].

Stalin had good reason to be satisfied with the results of the conference. In return for minor concessions – the acceptance of the United Nations and a future role for France in the councils of the great powers – he believed that the West had accepted Soviet control over Poland and Eastern Europe, although he recognised that this would have to be achieved behind a façade of self-determination. Roosevelt had said nothing at Yalta which disabused the Soviet leader of this impression. Stalin was willing to pay lip service to Western principles by encouraging the formation of so-called 'peoples' democracies' in Eastern Europe whereby communists formed coalition governments with anti-Nazi left and centrist parties. In countries under Red Army control real power of course rested with the communists although, for instance, in Czechoslovakia the collaboration between communist and non-communist parties was more genuine given the considerable pro-Soviet sympathies of a population which felt itself betrayed by the West in 1938. Stalin's efforts to contain the revolutionary zeal of the communists were not accomplished without difficulty: the Yugoslav communist partisans, led by Marshal Tito, had liberated Yugoslavia largely by their own efforts and had no intention of sharing power with the discredited pro-royalist party, while in China, American and

Soviet efforts to persuade Mao Tse-tung's communists to collaborate with Chiang Kai-shek's nationalists failed completely. In France, Italy and Belgium communist leaders accepted ministerial posts in coalition governments [47; 48].

For his part, Stalin had refrained from interference in areas of Europe which the Western powers had liberated during the war and he anticipated similar Western restraint towards Soviet-occupied Eastern Europe. The Allies, after defeating Italy and finally forcing the German armies in the north to capitulate in 1945, had administered the country with little or no consultation with the Soviet Union and Stalin had not raised any serious objection. Furthermore Stalin had lived up to his November 1944 agreement with Churchill and had given no support to the Greek communist and left-wing forces in their bitter struggle with the British-backed royalist government (although Tito did provide some aid to the communists across the Yugoslav border). Stalin considered that in these circumstances he could anticipate a free hand in Poland and he did nothing to prevent the subsequent refusal of the communist Polish provisional government to admit representatives of the London Poles. United States diplomats in other Eastern European countries were at the same time warning Washington that communist excesses hardly suggested that the Soviet Union intended to live up to her Yalta promises. Events in Poland led to a stream of complaints from Churchill to Roosevelt about Soviet perfidy and, by the end of March, even Roosevelt began to contemplate taking a harder line towards Moscow.

(iv) President Harry Truman and the Soviet Union

His death on 12 April 1945 meant that historians can only speculate as to how Roosevelt would have handled the problem. His successor, Harry S. Truman, a former Senator from Missouri, who had been chosen as a compromise vice-presidential candidate in 1944, had been kept in complete ignorance by Roosevelt about foreign policy. Roosevelt's dual policy of public rhetoric about the principles governing the post-war world and his private assurances to Stalin that he recognised Soviet security concerns was not understood by Truman, who while he promised to continue Roosevelt's policies, was unsure quite what these were.

His foreign policy advisers, men he had inherited from Roosevelt, were also divided about what course the new President should pursue. W. Averell Harriman, the United States ambassador to Moscow, who had returned home on hearing of Roosevelt's death, State Department officials, James F. Forrestal, the Navy Secretary, and Admiral William D. Leahy, the White House chief of staff, were all, in varying degrees, suspicious of Soviet policies and urged Truman to adopt a tough line towards Soviet violations of the Yalta accords. Henry L. Stimson, the War Secretary, Joseph E. Davies, a former pro-Soviet ambassador to Moscow, and General George C. Marshall, the Army Chief of Staff, pressed Truman on the other hand not to jeopardise the long-term prospects for Soviet-American co-operation for the sake of relatively minor Soviet transgressions in Eastern Europe, an area of little interest to the United States and where she was in any case powerless to influence the course of events. From London Truman was bombarded with telegrams from Churchill advocating a firm Anglo-American stand against the Soviet Union. Faced with this conflicting advice, Truman wavered. He was unwilling to adopt some of Churchill's more extreme suggestions, such as ordering Anglo-American forces to liberate Prague before the Russians arrived there, in order to prevent the communisation of Czechoslovakia. However, the President did remonstrate angrily with Molotov over Soviet violations of the Yalta agreements on Poland when the Soviet Foreign Minister visited Washington on 23 April on his way to the San Francisco Conference.

Truman soon realised that angry exchanges with Molotov were self-defeating, and by May he had reverted to Roosevelt's policy of conciliation. He believed that a direct appeal to Stalin about Poland over the heads of the supposedly hard-line Molotov and the Politburo might have more effect in changing Soviet policy. He sent Harry Hopkins, a close intimate of Roosevelt, who had used him as his personal emissary to Stalin during the war, to

Moscow (26 May–6 June) to suggest to the Soviet leader a Big Three meeting in the early summer, and also to reach a compromise over the vexed Polish question. This direct approach appeared to work: Stalin accepted a summit, agreed that the non-communist leaders would be given places in the Polish provisional government (and this took place on 21 June), repeated his Yalta promise of free elections in Poland and of Soviet entry into the war against Japan early in August. Churchill was irritated by Truman's *volte face* but had no alternative but to accept the results of the Hopkins mission and agree that the new Polish government should be recognised by the West once it had been reconstituted.

Despite this improvement in the atmosphere Truman remained at heart suspicious of Soviet policy, while Stalin, who had believed that he could work with Roosevelt, regarded Truman as an unknown quantity whose conduct so far towards the Soviet Union had been inconsistent. Truman's dilemma was that, given the rapid rundown in the numbers of American troops in Europe after Germany's surrender (some were transferred to the Far East, while others were being demobilised as quickly as possible to meet the growing clamour in the United States 'to bring the boys home'), the United States would soon have only a limited physical presence in Europe with which to back up its diplomacy [19; 24].

In these circumstances the only leverage available to the United States was its financial strength. In 1944 the American Treasury proposed that the United States offer the Soviet Union a loan to assist her post-war recovery and as evidence that the United States sought good relations with her. Stalin and Molotov expressed interest, and it also appealed to American business, attracted by the possibility that Soviet purchases of American industrial plant and the ensuing recovery of the Soviet economy would offer opportunities for expanded American trade in the Soviet Union at a time when economists were predicting a post-war US slump. After he became President, Truman's advisers suggested that this loan could be used to secure Soviet promises of good behaviour in Eastern Europe. Molotov's repeated suggestions for negotiations about a loan were either ignored or were answered by hints from Harriman that political conditions might be attached to it. American evasiveness on the subject and such attempts at blackmail increased Stalin's growing suspicion of Truman. A sudden end of lend-lease supplies on 7 May 1945, a result of Congressional pressure after the end of the war in Europe, (supplies for the Far East were continued until August), was bound to fuel Stalin's doubts, although it affected Great Britain as much as the Soviet Union. The loan scheme lapsed in the summer of 1945 [53]. However, a further means of influencing Soviet behaviour emerged on 25 April 1945 when Stimson acquainted Truman with the closely guarded secret of the Manhattan Project – the development, during the war, of the atomic bomb by a team of American, British and Canadian scientists – which was now approaching fruition. This was successfully tested in New Mexico in mid-July and the War Secretary expected to have at least two bombs available for use against Japan. Gar Alperovitz [4] has suggested that Truman's major preoccupation during the summer of 1945 was not the final defeat of Japan but the use of American possession of the bomb as a means of coercing the Soviet Union into adopting American policies in Eastern Europe and elsewhere. The sole motive for exploding the bombs on Japan, according to Alperovitz, was not to force the Japanese into surrender – he claims they were on the verge of defeat in any case – but to impress the Soviet Union with American possession of a weapon of such awesome power. This is a grotesque exaggeration. Although in hindsight it is true that the United States overestimated Japanese strength in early 1945, uppermost in Truman's mind at that time was that the use of the bomb would save countless American lives by forcing Japan into precipitate surrender.

The Japanese government had already put out peace feelers but it was doubted in Washington that that government was master in its own house. Moreover, no one could be sure in the spring of 1945 that the A-bomb would work, and Soviet intervention in the Far East was still considered crucial. However, undoubtedly some of Truman's advisers did think that the bomb would give the United States some bargaining strength in dealing with the Soviet Union. Truman's guarded hint to Stalin at the Potsdam Conference in July 1945 that the United States had successfully tested a weapon of great destructive power, was hardly likely to impress Stalin, whose non-committal reply concealed the fact that Soviet spies in the Western intelligence and scientific communities were keeping Moscow fully informed of the progress of the project. On returning to Moscow Stalin ordered the stepping up of Soviet efforts to produce a Russian nuclear weapon on which work had begun in earnest in 1942. United States employment of the A-bombs against the Japanese cities of Hiroshima and Nagasaki on 6 and 9 August 1945, which was followed by the Japanese surrender on the 15th, did not appear to have any effect on the course of Soviet policy. The Red Army entered the war as promised on 8 August and speedily overran Japanese positions in Manchuria. The Americans soon realised that their possession of the A-bomb gave them little diplomatic leverage to influence Soviet policy [45].

(v) The Potsdam Conference and after, July–December 1945

The Potsdam Conference of the three great powers (17 July–1 August 1945) did not produce any major constructive agreements but it did conceal temporarily the growing divergence between East and West. A reparations agreement was reached designed to reduce Soviet claims to German industrial capital in the three Western zones. Each occupying power was allowed to extract reparations freely from its own zone, while the Soviet Union was authorised to take 10 per cent from the Western zones, and a further 15 per cent provided that this was matched by supplies of food and raw materials from the Soviet zone. The Soviets again promised free elections in Poland. The United States finally accepted the Oder-Western Neisse line as Poland's future Western frontier. Substantive issues, such as the long-term future of Germany and peace treaties with Germany's former European allies (eventually signed in 1946) were referred to future meetings of the foreign ministers of the great powers for resolution.

Molotov demanded that the Montreux Convention, which restricted the passage of non-Turkish military vessels through the Dardanelles, should be scrapped and Soviet and other Black Sea countries should be allowed to use the Straits freely in future, while a joint Soviet-Turkish administration should replace the international regime of the Straits. Churchill had intimated in 1944, and again at Yalta, that the Straits regime might be altered in favour of Soviet Russia as Turkey had refused to join the Allies against Germany (she did not declare war until April 1945). He now regretted his premature enthusiasm, especially as Molotov linked his demands with a call for restoration to the Soviet Union of Turkish territory in the border provinces of Kars and Ardahan, ceded by the Soviet Republic to Turkey in 1921, and later pressed for Soviet naval bases in the Straits. These far-reaching demands only increased Western suspicions of Soviet policy towards Turkey. They were referred to the foreign ministers [20].

The problems of Italy and Romania were also aired at Potsdam, without any definite conclusion being reached. Both countries had switched sides during the war – Italy, after the overthrow of Mussolini in 1943 and the occupation of Southern Italy by the Western Allies, while Romania had been forced to declare war on Germany after the Red Army had entered the country in the following year. Both, however, were still regarded by the Allies as ex-enemy states.

Italy was governed largely by the British and American occupying forces through an Allied Control Commission, on which the Soviet Union had an advisory role, although in practice her presence was ignored. At the end of 1944 the Soviet Deputy Foreign Minister, Andrei Vyshinsky, visited Italy and helped to re-establish there a strong Communist Party, in the hope that the party would dominate a future Italian government when the constitution was restored. Beyond that, Stalin's Italian policy was obscure. Although Molotov protested at Potsdam about the Soviet Union's exclusion from the decision-making process in Italy, he did not press the matter. At the subsequent London Conference of foreign ministers he put forward a demand for $100 million in reparations from Italy, but Truman refused to lend Italy the money and the war-torn Italian economy was too impoverished to pay and the matter lapsed. Stalin was forced to move circumspectly – Yugoslavia wanted to annex Trieste, Italian since 1919, and defended in 1945 by Anglo-American troops. Stalin did not want to offend Tito by showing any support for Italy in the region. Italy remained in the Western camp after 1945, a result of the successful Allied defence of Trieste and generous American economic assistance.

Stalin used the West's refusal to allow the Soviet Union a voice in Italy to deny the Western Allies a say in the Control Commissions in Bulgaria, Hungary and Romania. In February 1945 Vyshinsky turned up in Bucharest and ordered King Michael to appoint a new pro-Soviet government dominated by the Communist Party. He warned the king that failure to do so might lead to the end of Romania's existence as an independent power and, on leaving, slammed the door so hard that the surrounding plaster cracked. In August the king tried to dismiss this government, invoking the Declaration on Liberated Europe and appealing to Britain and the United States for support. The West did nothing – Britain had no desire to disturb the 1944 percentages agreement with Stalin and risk interference in Greece, while Truman was indifferent to the question. In February 1946 the government was slightly enlarged by the addition of a few liberal politicians and, in return, the West agreed to recognise this new government. The change was purely cosmetic: the king was forced eventually to abdicate and the communists took over the country completely [4; 9].

During the conference Churchill and the British Foreign Secretary, Anthony Eden, were replaced by Clement Attlee and Ernest Bevin respectively as a result of the Labour Party's victory in the British general election in late July 1945. A number of the newly elected Labour Members of Parliament had been pro-communist in the 1930s, while John Strachey, a junior Air Minister, had been a Communist Party member before the war. Some left-wing MPs pressed the new government to renounce its ties with capitalist United States and throw in its lot with socialist Russia, but these were in the minority. In any case Attlee and Bevin were men of a different stamp. Neither shared the pro-communist or wartime sentimentality towards the Soviet Union of some of their supporters, although they made some half-hearted attempts to keep the wartime friendship with the Soviet Union alive. Although the Labour Party election manifesto attacked the anti-Soviet foreign policy of the Conservatives before 1939 and called for the continuation of the alliances with the United States and the Soviet Union into the peace, Attlee and Bevin had come to the conclusion that the Soviet Union was an imperialist power whose ambitions threatened the independence of Western Europe.

Publicly Bevin found it politically expedient to declare that a Labour government was much better placed than a Conservative one to work with Moscow but privately, as a former trade union leader and wartime Minister of Labour, he was well acquainted with the machinations and ambitions of domestic communists. Bevin's experiences with the intransigence of Molotov and other Soviet negotiators at Potsdam and later meetings convinced him that his assumptions about Soviet malevolence had been correct: he became as suspicious of Soviet policy as Churchill had been [13].

East–West relations experienced further deterioration during the autumn and winter of 1945 as the Soviet Union ignored Western protests about the ill-treatment of non-communist parties in Eastern Europe. The first post-war meeting of the Council of Foreign Ministers in London in September was the scene of angry accusations and counter-accusations. Molotov alleged British atrocities against Greek communists: Bevin condemned Soviet actions in Eastern Europe. The Soviets demanded a voice in the Allied occupation regimes in Italy and Japan, renewed their calls for the revision of the Montreux Convention and put forward a claim to a share in the trusteeship of Italy's former North African colony, Libya. Nor could any agreement be reached about the future of Germany – each side feared that a reunited Germany would fall under the other's influence. The occupation authorities had already started to treat their respective zones as their own separate satrapies, rendering the Potsdam agreement a dead letter. Indeed, the Yalta reparation accords hastened this tendency, as the Soviet Union began to extract the major share of her reparations claims from her own zone.

However, Truman's new Secretary of State, James F. Byrnes, still hoped for an agreement with the Soviet Union. Indeed Byrnes, whose reputation within the United States had been built up as a domestic conciliator, and who had been one of the two chief contenders for the vice-presidential nomination at the Democratic Party Convention in 1944 (from which Truman had emerged as the nominee), was convinced that he could achieve a working relationship with the Soviet Union by direct talks with the Soviet leaders. It was by now clear that American possession of the atomic bomb had had no impact on Soviet policy – if anything Molotov was even more obstinate at the London Conference than before. The Soviet demands in Turkey and Libya were put forward either as bargaining counters or to test Western will, but the Soviet Union also calculated that, since the United States was expanding her power worldwide, with bases in the Philippines and Japan, and had taken over Japan's former Pacific Island trusteeships in 1945, the Soviet Union, as a co-victor, had the right to achieve Russia's long-held ambition to secure unimpeded access to the Mediterranean. To the West, however, her demands appeared to be exorbitant, and they were bound to increase British anxiety about Soviet intentions in the Middle East and the Mediterranean, still a British preserve. Byrnes even suspected that the demand for a share in Libya's administration was part of a Soviet design to dominate Africa, and particularly the Belgian Congo, at that time the major source of the United States' uranium supply [45].

Soviet leaders were probably more concerned with the immense problems of trying to recover from the effects of war and occupation, with resources inadequate to the task, than with foreign policy issues. Moreover, the pressures of war had led to the rise of the Red Army, which had won much prestige in the Soviet Union as a result of its victories over Germany, of the heavy industrial sector under G.M. Malenkov, which had been expanded enormously to meet the needs of the war, and of the political police (the NKVD/

KGB) under L.B. Beria, which had accumulated vast powers during the war. Stalin feared that these powerful interests might challenge his authority, especially as the war had led to the weakening of Communist Party controls. In 1945 Stalin charged A.A. Zhadanov, a party activist and theoretician, with the task of reviving the influence of the party and countering the rising power of the military and industrial sectors [48].

These internal struggles, together with Stalin's fears of a new war, this time with the United States, were responsible for the cautious nature of his foreign policy, willing to test Western positions, yet receding if he met resistance, insisting on the Soviet Union's rights, yet uncertain of how to achieve them. Molotov's stubborn behaviour at the London Conference demonstrated the Soviet Union's determination to be treated as an equal by the West, and was designed to show that she was not to be overawed by the American monopoly of the atomic bomb [48].

However, the Soviet Union remained willing to take advantage of a more conciliatory approach, especially if this implied a rift in the Anglo-American relationship. Molotov accepted with alacrity a proposal by Byrnes that the three foreign ministers should meet in Moscow in December 1945. Britain was not consulted in advance about this initiative; plainly Byrnes hoped to reach agreement directly with Stalin and Molotov in Moscow. Bevin had no alternative but to attend the conference despite an earlier threat that he would stay away. At Moscow, after Byrnes had spoken to Stalin, the Soviet Union agreed that a Four-Power Control Commission should be sent to Romania to ensure non-communist representation in its government, while non-communists would be given posts in the Bulgarian government. In return, the United States agreed to set up an Allied Council in Tokyo to make suggestions to General MacArthur, the United States Supreme Commander in Japan, and virtual ruler of the country, about the occupation regime there. Finally it was agreed that the Council of Foreign Ministers would meet in the spring of 1946 to draw up peace treaties with Germany's former European allies.

These mutual concessions were purely cosmetic: the Western powers would continue to have as little influence in internal political arrangements in Romania as the Allied Council would have in Tokyo. Nevertheless the Moscow Conference led to a temporary thaw in American-Soviet relations. While determined to maintain Soviet control in Eastern Europe, Stalin had demonstrated a willingness to accept a façade of Allied co-operation in the area. Nor was Truman willing to consider a complete breach with the Soviet Union while there remained a chance, however slender, of a deal, despite his complaints that Byrnes had made too many concessions to the Soviet Union in Moscow. He was becoming increasingly aware that the public mood in the United States was beginning to turn against the Soviet Union, although it would not become completely anti-Soviet until the end of the following year. In November 1946 the Republicans, in the mid-term elections, gained control of both houses of Congress for the first time in eighteen years. Domestic considerations were the main factors in this victory, but nevertheless Republican Senators, such as former isolationist Arthur H. Vandenberg of Michigan, the Republican leader in the Senate, were becoming increasingly vocal in their attacks on Byrnes's alleged 'appeasement' of Moscow. While Truman was certainly irritated by Byrnes's failure to keep him properly informed about his initiatives in Moscow, all this did not mark a clear parting of the ways between East and West.

2 The Cold War becomes a Reality, 1946–1952

(i) Developments in 1946

The post-Moscow Conference thaw was short-lived. During 1946 there was a definite hardening of relations between the Soviet Union and the United States. By the following year a 'Cold War' had broken out which was to become the characteristic feature of East–West relations for the next two decades. The 'Cold War' was a state of continuing hostility and tension between the two world power blocs led by the United States and the Soviet Union. Before the advent of nuclear weapons the outcome of the bitter disputes between East and West, which spread from Europe to the Middle and Far East, would have been a major war. The possession of nuclear weapons of ever increasing and formidable power, and the appalling consequences of their use, did impose some restraint on the leaders of each side in their dealings with the other but, during the many confrontations between the two sides after 1946, the slightest miscalculation or over-reaction might well have led to catastrophe. The enormous power of the hydrogen bomb, which both sides developed in the early 1950s, imposed even greater caution on them, but even before 1949, when the United States alone possessed the atomic bomb, Truman was as reluctant to contemplate its use as Stalin was to provoke it.

Speeches by Stalin and other Soviet leaders in February 1946 warned the Soviet people that they were still threatened by capitalist encirclement and accused Western 'imperialists' of encouraging the formation of an anti-Soviet bloc. However, the main purpose of the speeches was to prepare the Soviet people for the heavy sacrifices which would result from the new Five Year Plans for the rebuilding of heavy industry and of Soviet military strength. Furthermore, Molotov distinguished between the majority of peace-loving peoples of the world and the small group of reactionary elements in the West who sought renewed conflict – a hint that, if the peaceful majority exerted itself, co-existence was still possible [48].

Neither side had any real reason to fear the other in 1946. American army strength by March 1946 had fallen to 400,000 from a peak of 3.5 million in May 1945. The United States lacked sufficient atomic bombs to inflict a decisive blow on the Soviet Union. In any case, despite a marked decline in earlier pro-Soviet sentiment, the American people were unlikely to support a new conflict so soon after the end of the Second World War. American intelligence was well aware that the devastation inflicted on the Soviet economy by four years of ruinous war made it impossible for her to contemplate fresh hostilities: nor of course did Stalin seek a conflict. American attention focused more on the dangers posed by the strong communist parties in Western Europe, which thrived on conditions of acute economic and political instability. Some alarm was expressed at the presence of twenty Red Army divisions in Central Europe at a time when Western Europe's defences barely existed. Total Red Army strength was put at about 2.5 million in 1946. This was an exaggeration: the Soviet Union had also demobilised rapidly after 1945 in order to release manpower for industrial reconstruction, and the size and strength of each Red Army division was overestimated, as American analysts recognised later [63].

That United States opinion was not yet prepared to regard the Soviet Union as an implacable enemy was shown by the hostile reception in the United States of a speech by Winston Churchill, now leader of the British opposition, at Fulton, Missouri, on 5 March 1946, in which he talked of an 'iron curtain' having 'descended across the Continent [of Europe] from Stettin in the Baltic to Trieste in the Adriatic' and appealed for a renewal of the wartime Anglo-American alliance as a means of deterring Soviet expansionism. Truman, who had read the speech prior to its delivery, and was present at the address, subsequently disassociated himself from it [30]. Some of the protests were the product of suspicions that Churchill sought United States assistance to maintain the British Empire, while British efforts to deal even-handedly between the Arabs and Jews in the strife-torn British-mandated territory of Palestine created even further hostility towards her in the United States, where the powerful Jewish lobby accused the British of favouring the Arab cause. In December 1945 much bitterness was occasioned in Britain over negotiations for a much needed American loan of $3.75 billion. The terms of this loan were not onerous, but one of the conditions was that Britain should abolish commonwealth preferences and restore sterling to full convertibility by 1947, thus encouraging the expansion of American controls over Britain and her empire. This led to angry protests from both right- and left-wing MPs in the House of Commons about the implications for British interests and sovereignty of such a clause. The Americans also began to recede from Roosevelt's wartime pledge that Britain and Canada should receive full information about America's atomic programme after the war. In 1946 the McMahon Act resulted in a permanent ban on such information. From 1946 the British began to develop their own atomic bomb [8; 9; 13].

However, the steady deterioration in Soviet-American relations overshadowed these Anglo-American quarrels. In Germany mounting American irritation with Soviet and French reparations seizures in the United States zone led the United States army to suspend Soviet reparations deliveries on 3 May. The transfer of German industrial plant to the East threatened to wreck the economy of West Germany completely. Foreign Ministers Conferences in April, June and July 1946 deadlocked over the future of Germany. The West suspected that the Soviets only wanted a unified Germany if it was under communist domination. The Soviets accused the United States of seeking a Germany tied economically and militarily to the West. There were endless arguments about the levels of industrial production Germany should be permitted to achieve, with the Soviet Union and France (who both had good reasons to fear a resurgent Germany) pressing for the pegging of German steel and other industrial

36

production at a low level to prevent the revival of a German armaments industry. They also called for Franco-Soviet participation in an international authority to control the Ruhr, Germany's main industrial base. By 1946 Britain and the United States had concluded that the economic recovery of Western Europe as a whole depended on the rehabilitation of the German industries. While they were willing to provide safeguards against the re-emergence of a German military threat, including a 25-year, four-power treaty to guarantee the disarmament of the country (which the Soviets rejected), they opposed efforts to impose harsh controls on Germany's peaceful economic revival. The division of Germany into two hostile camps became more marked as both sides began to encourage the revival of German political parties on a local level in their zones. In East Germany the non-communist socialist party was merged into a communist front organisation (the Socialist Unity Party). Separatist tendencies in the West were enhanced when, on 6 September 1946, in a speech at Stuttgart, Byrnes reassured his German audience that the United States would not withdraw her occupation forces from West Germany in the foreseeable future. He stated that the United States would continue to support the reunification of Germany. If this should prove impossible, she intended to encourage the revival of the West German economy. Then, on 1 January 1947, Britain, economically exhausted and unable to continue to bear alone the burden of sustaining her zone, agreed to merge it with the American zone.

Events outside Europe created additional tensions. In 1942 the Soviet Union had occupied north Iran and Britain the south in order to prevent crucial Iranian oil resources falling to the Nazis, and to render it secure as an overland route for the passage of lend-lease supplies to the Soviet Union. Both powers had promised to withdraw their troops six months after the end of the war. On 15 March 1946 the British duly withdrew their forces but the Red Army in the north showed no sign of following suit. There were fears that the Soviet Union sought to annex the Iranian province of Azerbaijan and there were ominous reports of Soviet troop movement along the borders of Iran. The Soviet Union now began to demand that Teheran agree to grant Soviet agencies oil concessions in the north. Undoubtedly Stalin overplayed his hand. The Iranian government was not ill-disposed towards the Soviet Union, while Moscow felt that she had as much right to oil concessions in the north as Britain had to her valuable oil fields in the south. But the threatening behaviour of the Soviet Union led the State Department to suspect that the Russians were seeking to dominate Iran. Moreover, the United States was no longer self-sufficient in oil and insisted that the oil reserves of the Middle East must be kept out of hostile control. Byrnes, now converted by Truman and Republican leaders to a hard line, made a fuss about the Soviet actions in both the United Nations and in protest notes to Moscow. Finally the Soviet Union withdrew her troops from North Iran in May, having extracted oil concessions from the Iranian government (which were subsequently repudiated by the Iranian Parliament) and restored Azerbaijan to full Iranian sovereignty. Truman was now convinced that a policy of firmness towards the Soviet Union paid dividends, while Soviet probing for advantage in Iran reinforced his suspicions of their motives [41].

Mutual suspicions also wrecked efforts to reach East–West agreement on the control of the atomic bomb. In 1945 Stimson, the War Secretary, had urged Truman to place the atomic secret under joint Soviet-American control. He argued that the Soviets were bound eventually to develop their own bomb: it would be better to anticipate the ending of the American monopoly by an early international agreement to neutralise this devastating weapon. A United States plan (the so-called Baruch plan) to place atomic raw materials and their inspection under a United Nations control agency, which would not be subject to the veto, foundered on the Soviet accusation that she would be prevented from developing her own nuclear capability, and her territory subjected to inspection, while the United States would retain her monopoly over the bomb during the formative years of the agency. A Soviet proposal to ban the production of nuclear weapons and the destruction of existing stockpiles was rejected by the United States. This debate, which took place during late 1946 in the newly created United Nations Atomic Energy Commission, was the precursor of long and futile East–West disarmament negotiations in which propaganda and Cold War rhetoric replaced any meaningful search for arms control [32; 46].

Hard-line elements in the American nuclear and military establishments were opposed to any tampering with their nuclear monopoly. They believed that even if Soviet scientists knew how to produce atomic bombs, American control of the world's main uranium deposits in the Belgian Congo, together with the Soviet Union's lack of technological expertise and of the expensive facilities needed to manufacture them would retard a Soviet bomb for years. Truman accepted these arguments, the more so as he no longer felt it was possible to trust the Soviet Union.

(ii) The Truman Doctrine and the Marshall Plan

In 1947 Truman inaugurated the 'containment' of Soviet expansionism and ended the hesitancy which had character-ised American policy towards the Soviet Union since 1945. Those Cabinet members who continued to believe that compromise was possible were eased out of office. Such was the fate of Henry A. Wallace, a former Vice President and now Commerce Secretary, who was forced to resign in September 1946, after a speech in New York in which he called for a renewed effort to achieve a Soviet-American agreement. James Byrnes, whom Truman considered too soft towards the Soviet Union, was replaced as Secretary of State in January 1947 by General George C. Marshall, the wartime Army Chief-of-Staff. Moreover, political considerations forced Truman to conclude that there could be no meaningful negotiations with the Soviet Union in 1947. After the November 1946 Republican victories in the Congressional elections, Truman's legislation was dependent on the votes of staunchly anti-communist Republicans who, paradoxically, sought to curb government expenditure and lower taxation. Truman would have to dwell upon Soviet hostility if he was to persuade these senators to vote extra money for defence and overseas expenditures.   The most dramatic indication of the Truman administration's new hard-line policy towards communism was its decision to take over Britain's responsibilities for meeting the military costs of the Greek government's military campaign against Greek communist insurgents. The government, despite this aid and the assistance of British troops, had been unable to prevent the insurgents from securing control over the bulk of the Greek hinterland by 1947. The British government, weary of the instability and corruption of the Greek anti-communist coalition, and faced with its own grave financial problems in early 1947, announced on 1 February that it could no longer afford to subsidise either the Greek or the Turkish armies (the Turkish army had been permanently mobilised since 1945 in the face of the Soviet threat to the Straits), and was withdrawing all support to them on 31 March 1947. The Greek insurgents were supported by Tito's Yugoslavia and by Bulgaria and, while there is some evidence that Stalin did not wholeheartedly back Tito's ambitions in Greek Macedonia – he did not approve of Tito's schemes for a Balkan federation – the Americans believed Moscow would welcome a communist-controlled Greece if, as seemed likely, the royalist government collapsed. While already aware of Britain's reluctance to continue propping up the Greeks, Washington was caught off balance by Britain's sudden announcement of her intention to withdraw from the Eastern Mediterranean. Nonetheless it provided Truman and his Under Secretary of State, Dean Acheson, with the opportunity to extend American protection to Greece and Turkey.

Aware of the difficulty of persuading cost-conscious Republican Senators to vote the sums necessary to succour Greece and Turkey, Truman and Acheson emphasised the communist danger, painting in lurid colours the likely spread of communist regimes in Western Europe and the Middle East if Greece and Turkey succumbed. This alarmist talk resulted in the passage of an aid bill for Greece and Turkey through Congress in May, preceded by the President's enunciation of the famous 'Truman Doctrine', promising that the United States would 'support free peoples who are resisting subjugation by armed minorities or outside pressures'. This vision of a worldwide communist conspiracy, however much it

40

impressed American legislators, appeared to commit the United States to a universal crusade to eradicate the menace, although Acheson insisted that the United States would act only in cases where her vital interests were at stake [2; 5].

The Greek communist insurgents were eventually defeated by the Greek army, with the help of American aid and military advisers. The United States next turned her attention to war-ravaged Western Europe. The new American Secretary of State, Marshall, returning via Western Europe to Washington from an abortive Foreign Ministers Conference in Moscow in the spring of 1947, was appalled at the economic and social distress he witnessed in Europe. The West European economies were suffering acute balance of payments difficulties caused by the need to spend scarce dollars to pay for essential imports of food and raw materials from the United States. At the same time their industrial and agricultural production languished because of a shortage of investment funds. The harsh winter of 1947 had exacerbated their difficulties by causing a severe fuel crisis and a breakdown in communications. The United Kingdom had practically exhausted the 1945 American loan, and her resumption of full sterling convertibility on 15 July 1947 led to such a drain on her meagre reserves that she was forced to suspend it on 20 August 1947.

Marshall and his advisers feared that unless generous American aid to Europe was provided soon the deterioration in the economic life of Western Europe would lead to a severe slump which would have dire effects on the American economy. An economic crisis of such magnitude might encourage the peoples of Western Europe to turn to communism and the Soviet Union for their salvation – the communist parties in France and Italy had already attracted considerable electoral support and communists occupied ministerial posts in their coalition governments.

In a speech at Harvard University on 5 June 1947 Marshall called for a determined United States effort to promote the economic revival of Europe and thus ensure the continued prosperity of the American economy. He suggested that the European governments confer about their respective financial problems and then approach the United States with

41

a common programme, setting out the dollar aid they would require to rectify their trade imbalances with the United States, which would enable them to release funds for investment and recovery. An additional invitation was extended to the Soviet Union and the Central and East European states, although the State Department hoped that it would be refused. In view of the growing hostility in the United States towards the Soviet Union it was not very likely that Congress would have approved the vast sums the shattered Soviet economy required, or indeed would have passed the programme at all if it had been linked to massive aid to the Soviet Union. Molotov and a team of 89 Soviet economic experts turned up at the preliminary conference of the European powers in Paris on 26 June 1947, called to draw up Marshall Plan requirements, in order to discover the terms on which United States aid to the Soviet Union might be available. However, he soon abandoned the meeting, refusing to supply the economic data on which Washington insisted before credits could be extended. Czechoslovakia, which had agreed to attend a further European conference on the aid plan on 7 July 1947, was ordered by Moscow to withdraw her acceptance [5].

The episode does suggest, however, that Stalin – who had assured a visiting American politician in April 1947 that he was still willing to do business with the United States – had not finally determined on a breach with the United States at this time. Yet he could not afford to open the Soviet Union to the prying eyes of Marshall Aid planners. A society which was making heavy sacrifices to rebuild Soviet industry, and which suffered a serious harvest failure in 1946, had to be sealed off from Western influences. In 1946–7 the Soviet Communist Party launched a vicious campaign against foreign and bourgeois literature, thus reversing the relaxation in cultural controls which had taken place during the war [48].

The Western European powers drew up their Marshall Plan requirements, and after complicated negotiations they were accepted by the United States. In 1948 Truman was able to persuade Congress to provide the necessary funds under the European Recovery Act, a task assisted by a complete communist take-over of power in Czechoslovakia in February 1948, which further fuelled anti-Soviet feelings in Congress.

The Czechoslovakian coup was the final act in the reversal of the Kremlin's policy of encouraging the formation of peoples' democracies in Eastern Europe. In 1946 and 1947 the left-wing coalitions in the region were gradually replaced by communist governments and communist collaboration with centre-left governments in Western Europe was brought to an end. With the definite emergence of two blocs in Europe, Stalin sought to bring the European communist parties, and particularly Tito's Yugoslavia which was demonstrating an unwanted independence, more firmly under Moscow's control. At a meeting of the nine European communist parties in Polish Silesia from 22 to 27 September 1947 the first steps in this direction were taken by the establishment of the Communist Information Bureau, designed to provide more direct channels of communication between the Soviet and other communist parties. Zhadanov bitterly attacked Western imperialists and capitalists and called for an energetic communist propaganda campaign against warmongers. During the autumn of 1947 Western communist parties were instructed to do all in their power to bring down their governments and a wave of strikes and demonstrations against the Marshall Plan was launched. The Soviet Union hoped that this pressure upon the wavering and insecure coalition governments, particularly in France and Italy, would lead to their downfall and replacement by communist-dominated governments who would renounce both the Marshall Plan and reliance upon the United States and throw in their lot with the Soviet bloc. Thus domestic upheaval and revolution would lead to far-reaching changes in the foreign orientation of Western European countries [48].

The centre-left government of Italy managed to weather the storm, assisted by timely and much publicised injections of emergency United States aid coupled with American threats to cut off all financial assistance to Italy if the country succumbed to communism, and rumours of possible American military intervention if she did so. The French government's resistance to the communist-inspired strikes and riots was also bolstered by American aid, but it was a close-run thing: many foreign observers feared that the country would become ungovernable and therefore ripe for a communist coup. The Dutch and Belgian governments had less difficulty in riding the storm. No doubt the communist-inspired violence and intimidation were in the end counter-productive, alienating the moderate elements in the West European populations which might otherwise have been more sympathetic to communist propaganda against American imperialism. They were driven into the arms of the propertied classes in defence of law and order. In the aftermath the Western communist parties and their mentor, the Soviet Union, lost a considerable amount of credibility and prestige in the eyes of former sympathisers and the uncommitted. The reputation for respectability and responsibility which they had tried to build up after 1945 was destroyed.

(iii) The Berlin blockade and the formation of NATO, 1948–9

The Soviet Union also reacted angrily to developments in Western Germany where the merged British and American zones (France did not agree to merge her zone with theirs until March 1948) were moving towards the creation of an administration in which the German non-communist political parties would have a major role, with the object of formulating a federal constitution for the area. Another meeting of Western and Soviet foreign ministers in November and December 1947 produced no agreement on the future of Germany, and Stalin decided to take more direct action to force the West to reverse its German policy. Berlin had been divided into four military sectors in 1945, reflecting the zonal division of Germany, but it was supposed to be governed as an entity by the four Allied military commanders. The three Western sectors of the city were isolated deep within the Soviet zone of Germany, with long road and rail communications to the Western zones. The communications were under Soviet control and were not subject to any clear Western-Soviet agreement about access rights. Moscow's

44

decision to cut off all road and rail traffic between West Berlin and the Western zones of Germany on 24 July 1948 was the culmination of weeks of sporadic interference with Western access to the city. The Soviet action was precipitated by the West's decision to introduce a new West German currency as the first step towards the rejuvenation of the West German economy, and a dispute with the Soviets over whether this currency should circulate in Berlin.

Larger issues were of course at stake. The Soviet Union was becoming increasingly alarmed as the West pursued the separate development of Western Germany, which pointed towards the creation of a sovereign and remilitarised West German state. Soviet pressure on West Berlin was designed to persuade the West to abandon its plans for Western Germany or, if this failed, to force the West to quit Berlin while the Soviet Union built up a separate East German state tied to Moscow politically and militarily. In this situation the presence of a relatively prosperous Western bastion in the former German capital, in the heart of Eastern Germany, was an embarrassment. Further more, the knowledge that the West was prepared to abandon the West Berliners to their fate would cause the West Germans to pause before they associated themselves too closely with the Western powers.

Truman was determined that the West should not be driven out of Berlin by Soviet pressure. He did, however, reject a proposal by General Lucius D. Clay, the United States Military Governor of Germany, that an Allied convoy under military protection should attempt to force a passage to West Berlin. The President was anxious to avoid a confrontation which might escalate into all-out war. His advisers agreed upon a less provocative solution and from July 1948 to May 1949, when both the Berlin blockade and an Allied counter-blockade of the Soviet zone were ended, an Anglo-American airlift managed to keep the West Berliners supplied with basic fuel and food requirements. Despite a number of incidents the Soviets did not interfere with the airlift. Indeed, as a warning to the Soviet Union, Truman authorised the despatch of B-29 heavy bombers, capable of striking targets within the Soviet Union, to British bases in

July 1948. Although these bombers were not modified to enable them to carry atomic bombs, Stalin's decision to call off the blockade demonstrated the failure of the Soviet Union to achieve any of its objectives. He had not called it off before in the hope that continued pressure on West Berlin might still split the three Western powers and lead them to make some concessions. He also wanted to avoid a too precipitate and humiliating Soviet climbdown. The West did, however, agree to hold another Foreign Ministers Conference in May and June 1949 to discuss the future of Germany – a meeting which was as futile as its predecessors [5].

Indeed, the Berlin confrontation was, from the Soviet point of view, counter-productive. It increased Western alarm about Stalin's ultimate intentions and focused their attention more closely on the vulnerability of Western Europe to a Soviet attack. In the event of a war the United States and Britain planned to bomb Soviet cities and industries from bases in Britain and the Middle East, using both conventional and atomic weapons. However, this would not prevent the Red Army from brushing aside the weak Western European defences and occupying the area – indeed, the British and Americans planned to evacuate their occupation troops in Germany to Britain should the Soviet Union invade Western Europe. The Berlin crisis prompted the Western European states to improve their defence. In March 1948 Britain, France, the Netherlands, Belgium and Luxembourg had signed the Brussels Pact, which provided for mutual action in the event of aggression against any of the signatories. The Brussels Treaty powers promised to co-ordinate and plan their defences in advance. However, it was clear from the outset that without the material and psychological support of the United States, the relatively weak Western European states would never be able to build up their forces sufficiently to mount a credible deterrent to the Soviet Union.

The Truman administration was willing to further its increasing commitment to West European stability by contributing directly to the defence of the area. Stalin's Berlin blockade had convinced some previously sceptical Senators that the Soviet Union was a major threat to world peace, and they were now willing to jettison their isolationist sentiments and support a United States initiative in Western Europe. Supported by Republican and Democratic Senators, the Republican leader, Arthur H. Vandenberg, successfully secured the passage through the Senate of the famous 'Vandenberg Resolution' on 11 June 1948, which authorised the United States to enter into alliances with non-American powers. Negotiations were brought to a successful conclusion in April 1949 when the Brussels powers, together with the United States, Canada, Denmark, Iceland, Italy, Portugal and Norway, signed the North Atlantic Treaty, which provided for mutual defence in the case of an attack on one or more of the signatories by the Soviet Union. Greece and Turkey joined the organisation in 1952. An accompanying military aid bill provided for American military assistance to the West European armies. The ratification of this treaty by the United States still required the consent of two-thirds of the Senate and many Senators doubted that United States security required participation in such a far-reaching pact, while others were reluctant to vote for the accompanying aid bill. Acheson persuaded many of the waverers to vote for both the Treaty and the aid bill by convincing them that the Treaty would not require the despatch of any more American troops to Europe. This promise returned to haunt the administration during the Korean War. He also insisted that the Treaty was based on the principle of mutual aid – that United States financial assistance was intended to help the Europeans to build up their own arms industries and armies and make them less dependent on the United States in the future. The Senate therefore consented to the Treaty in July 1949, but many Senators were given the impression that it was only intended to boost West European morale and encourage self-help, and thus would require few United States sacrifices beyond the initial financial outlay [34].

(vi) Cold War developments in 1949

American satisfaction with developments in Western Europe was soon overshadowed by the startling revelation that the Soviet Union had exploded an atomic bomb in August 1949.

The loss of the United States atomic monopoly, years earlier than many of her scientists had forecast, coupled with the communist victory in China over Chiang Kai-shek's nationalist (Kuomintang) forces in the autumn, seemed alarming indications that communism was on the march everywhere. Truman had long since abandoned any hope that the corrupt and incompetent Kuomintang regime would defeat the communists in the Chinese civil war, and had no intention of committing United States troops to the nationalist side, although Chiang received United States financial aid and military equipment. Soon the legend gained ground in the Republican Party – assisted by Kuomintang propaganda in the United States – that Truman had abandoned Chiang to his fate: 400 million Chinese had been 'lost' to 'godless communism'.

The shocks inflicted on American self-confidence by these events resulted in a marked shift in the attitude of public opinion towards communism. Hitherto Americans had accepted the need to contain the Soviet Union in Europe and the Middle East fairly calmly – the situation called for firmness rather than for drastic measures and military budgets remained at a fairly low level in these years. After 1949 attention shifted to the Far East, traditionally an area of American concern, and where it now appeared that communism had achieved a major triumph. To apply the containment doctrine to this vast region was a much more complex and hazardous undertaking than in Europe: most Asian societies and governments were unstable and even turbulent, while intense nationalism might ally with, rather than against, communism in the face of 'Western imperialism', which for many was a recent and bitter memory.

The Chinese communist victory, coupled with the Soviet explosion of an atomic bomb (which demonstrated that Soviet technology was not as backward as many had assumed) had an unsettling effect on American society. 'Isolationism' in the traditional sense had all but disappeared. The United States could no longer insulate herself militarily from the rest of the world. The Atlantic and Pacific Oceans were no longer secure moats behind which the United States would have time to build up her immense potential to defeat an aggressor.

Nor could the West Europeans hope to delay an invasion from the East for a sufficient period to enable the United States to complete her preparations. However, the rise of communism in China, a country in which the United States had strong ties of sentiment resulting from intense American missionary and economic activity there, led to the formation of a powerful 'China Lobby' in the Republican Party, which called for a concentration of American resources in future on an 'Asia First' strategy, with assistance to Europe reduced to an absolute minimum. At the same time the discovery of a number of spies in the Canadian and British scientific establishments led to suspicions that the Soviet atomic bomb resulted not from her own scientific expertise but from treachery in the West. In the same way the fall of the nationalist Chinese was attributed to the activities of pro-Chinese communist traitors inside the State Department and diplomatic service. The ensuing fuss forced Truman to authorise loyalty investigations of prominent public servants – the only crime of many having been to extol the virtues of the Soviet alliance when it had been fashionable to do so during the war. This was to be the precursor of a more deadly and thorough-going anti-communist witch hunt in the 1950s.

Truman ordered the crash development of the hydrogen (H) bomb – enormously more destructive than the atomic bomb – and set up a joint State and Defence Department committee to investigate the state of United States defences in the aftermath of the explosion of the Soviet atomic device. This investigation was carried out under the auspices of the National Security Council (NSC), set up in 1947 to co-ordinate American defence and foreign policies. The ensuing report, filed as NSC 68, expressed in the most alarmist terms the worldwide threat posed by communism to the free world. It recommended that American military capabilities – both nuclear and conventional – be expanded so that the United States could deal with communist challenges wherever and in whatsoever form they manifested themselves. This rearmament programme should be completed by 1954 when the committee prophesied that the Soviet Union, which devoted a far larger proportion of its Gross National Product

(GNP) to defence than the United States, would be fully capable of deploying nuclear weapons in a war with the West [63].

Truman wanted to keep arms expenditure as low as possible and he ignored the report. He accepted the air force view that air power, together with the vast potential power of the H-bomb, would be sufficient to deter Soviet aggression. He did authorise increased expenditure on nuclear and bomber development. Nor was he prepared to over-react to the establishment of Mao Tse-tung's communist regime in mainland China. Dean Acheson, now Secretary of State, expected that the island of Formosa (Taiwan), whither Chiang's forces had fled from the mainland after their defeat, would soon fall to the communists and he had no intention of trying to prevent a communist seizure of the island. In a speech in January 1950 Acheson stated that American security in the Pacific region depended on her bases on the island chain running from the Aleutian Islands through Okinawa and Japan to the Philippines. By implication Korea was excluded from this defence perimeter [50].

Stalin's reaction to the emergence of a new communist power in China was ambiguous. Publicly the Soviet Union welcomed the communist victory, but Stalin had done very little to help Mao's cause. When Stalin quarrelled with Tito in 1947 over Yugloslavia's scheme to set up a South Slav federation with Bulgaria, which resulted in Yugoslavia's expulsion from the Soviet bloc, he had been reluctant to unleash the Red Army against Yugoslavia which possessed an army of seasoned Second World War veterans. He had good reason to feel apprehensive about the rise of an even more independent communist state in China which might eventually rival the Soviet Union. The weak nationalist government of Chiang Kai-shek was preferable, in Soviet eyes, to a stronger communist regime. Soon Mao began to demand, and eventually achieved, the restoration of the territorial and economic concessions Stalin had wrested from the nationalists in 1945.

In 1949 a new wave of purges of both the Communist Party of the Soviet Union and those of Eastern and Central Europe showed that Stalin was determined to enforce his will inside the Soviet Union and to consolidate Moscow's control over the satellite states. Only rigid Stalinists who would not deviate from the Kremlin line remained in office. However, for the foreseeable future, Stalin could rely on Mao Tse-tung's loyalty – China was dependent on Soviet military, material and moral support, especially as the United States refused to have any dealings with the Peking regime. During a visit to Moscow in early 1950 Mao signed a treaty of mutual assistance with the Soviet Union, directed against Japan, and secured Soviet credits and material assistance [49].

(v) The Korean War, 1950–1953

On 25 June 1950 the armed forces of the Communist ruler of North Korea, Kim Il Sung, launched a surprise attack on the Republic of (South) Korea, an invasion which Stalin supported. Korea had been liberated from the Japanese, who had annexed the country in 1910, by the Red Army in 1945. The Soviet Union and the United States had divided Korea between them for military purposes at the 38th parallel in the same year, with the Red Army occupying the north and the United States the south. Subsequent efforts to reunite the country had fallen foul of the growing antipathy between the occupying powers and, as a result, two separate regimes had developed in the country. After 1946 the Soviets sent military aid and advisers to build up Kim Il Sung's army while the United States, which had withdrawn its troops from the south in 1948, provided military and economic aid to the ruler of South Korea, Syngman Rhee. Stalin did not believe that the United States would intervene to save Rhee's dictatorial and corrupt regime. The United States did not have a formal treaty of alliance with South Korea and, moreover, Acheson had excluded the country from the United States defence perimeter in January 1950. A communist-controlled South Korea, close to the Japanese mainland, would encourage Tokyo to adopt a neutral stance in the East–West struggle. Mao, preoccupied by domestic problems and with preparing his forces for an invasion of Formosa,

51

was in no position to oppose the invasion.

Truman ordered American air and naval forces in the vicinity to assist Rhee's forces and shortly thereafter United States army units from Japan helped the beleaguered South Koreans. In the absence of the Soviet delegate, who had boycotted the United Nations Security Council since January 1950 in protest at the non-admission of communist China to the organisation, Truman secured the passage of two United Nations resolutions at the end of June and in early July condemning North Korea for her aggression and calling on United Nations members to assist South Korea. Some of America's allies, such as Britain and France, sent token ground forces, but the bulk of the subsequent fighting was undertaken by South Korean and United States troops, under the command of General Douglas MacArthur, the commander of United States forces in the Far East.

After a dramatic United Nations landing at Inchon, on the west coast of North Korea, on 15 September 1950, the communist advance was reversed and soon the North Korean army was in full retreat across the 38th parallel. Truman authorised MacArthur to cross the parallel with the object of unifying Korea under United Nations auspices. The United Nations advance towards the Yalu River, the border between North Korea and Chinese Manchuria, led Mao to send Chinese communist troops in the guise of 'volunteers' to help the North Koreans. Despite both UN and US assurances that their forces would remain on Korean soil only until Korea had been reunified, Mao could not tolerate the presence of American troops on the frontiers of China. By December 1950–January 1951 MacArthur's forces were once more driven back deep into South Korea, and Britain urged the United States, faced with the possible evacuation of United Nations forces from Korea, not to widen the war by bombing China as MacArthur was demanding. London feared that such action would bring in the Soviet Union on China's side in the struggle and that the ensuing war would be worldwide. In March 1951 United Nations forces launched a counter-offensive which brought them back to the 38th parallel and bitter fighting thereafter failed to remove this frontier more than a few miles in either direction. So frustrated was MacArthur by the stalemate that in April 1951 he resumed his demand – this time publicly – for the air force to be authorised to bomb China, with nuclear weapons if necessary. Faced with this challenge, both to his authority as commander-in-chief and to his limited war strategy, Truman dismissed the general from all his commands in the Far East [31; 44].

The Korean War, and particularly the United Nations invasion of North Korea, intensified the Cold War. Truman adopted the provisions of NSC 68 and ordered a major rearmament programme. Britain and France followed suit. While the Anglo-French programmes produced improved weapons and equipment for their troops, they had only a marginal effect on the defence of Western Europe. Most of France's military resources were channelled into Indochina, where her generals were planning a new offensive against the communist insurgents: she had few troops left over to augment her NATO forces. Britain too, saddled with worldwide military commitments, was equally in no position to spare additional manpower for European defence. In any case her rearmament programme was soon cut back when it resulted in increasing economic and financial difficulties. Inevitably the situation led to mounting American pressure on her allies to utilise West German manpower and industrial resources for military purposes.

Many Western defence analysts suspected that the Soviet-backed North Korean invasion of the South was a feint designed to divert American attention (and resources) from Europe, thus enabling the Soviets to force the inadequately prepared West Europeans into the Soviet bloc. While this was an exaggeration, no doubt Stalin anticipated that events in the Far East would lead to the relaxation of United States vigilance in Europe, enabling him to extract concessions in Germany or Berlin.

Inevitably the crisis in Korea strengthened the pressure of the 'China Lobby' on Truman to switch to an 'Asia First' strategy, and of course MacArthur was a leading proponent of this view. Truman believed that to adopt this strategy would result in the United States being pinned down by a secondary enemy, China, in the Far East, while the main enemy, the Soviet Union, forced her will on Western Europe. Accordingly he strengthened both theatres in 1950 and 1951. United States reinforcements were despatched to Korea while the administration decided to give Chiang Kai-shek military and financial support and moved the United States navy into the Formosa Straits to deter the Chinese communists from attacking Formosa – at the same time it prevented the nationalists from invading the mainland [31; 44]. In 1951 a peace treaty was signed with Japan which tied Japan to the United States and allowed American troops to remain in Okinawa. Finally, the United States agreed to provide military assistance in 1950 to the French in Indochina. Since 1945, when their colonial possession had been restored to them, the French had been engaged in a bitter guerrilla struggle with Ho Chi Minh's communist (Vietminh) forces for control of the country. Ho was a nationalist as much as a communist, but the decision of both Moscow and Peking to recognise his movement as the legitimate government of Indochina and to provide him with aid in 1950 convinced the United States that he was an agent of the Kremlin [50].

(vi) The recovery of West Germany

In 1951 Truman authorised the despatch of an additional four divisions of American troops to West Germany to bolster Western European defences. Many Senators were angered by this decision – they had been assured by Acheson in 1949 that the NATO treaty would not lead to a further American troop commitment to Europe. At the same time the administration began to press for the rearmament of West Germany. Since the formation of NATO the United States Department of Defense (Pentagon) had believed that the West Europeans would need to build up their forces to provide 35–40 divisions as a credible deterrent to a Soviet land invasion. However, the Europeans were unwilling to make the sacrifices necessary to achieve such a force level. Furthermore the NATO planners wanted the West European defence line moved forward from its 1950 position on the River Rhine further east to Western Germany's frontier near the Elbe, so that the resources of West Germany would remain available to the West in the event of a Soviet attack. This would also provide NATO with greater defensive depth. Given the failure of the other European powers to expand their own forces sufficiently to defend this enlarged area, Washington demanded the utilisation of West German manpower to fill the gap. This pressure was strenuously resisted by the French, fearful of the resurgence of German military power.

After the end of the war France had demanded the imposition of severe reparations burdens on Germany and had resisted Anglo-American efforts to encourage the expansion of Germany's industrial production. For the most part these French aims had been frustrated. Reparations in the Western zones had been abandoned by 1948, and coal, iron and steel production began to expand dramatically after 1949 when West Germany received Marshall Aid funds. In 1949 a West German federal government had been established and its Chancellor, Konrad Adenauer, was pressing for full sovereign rights. The French now attempted to secure West Germany's co-operation to prevent the rise of unrestrained German industrial power. In 1950 the French government put forward the Schuman Plan for a European Coal and Steel Community, to consist of France, West Germany, the Benelux countries and Italy. This French project, while establishing global production targets for these commodities, would regulate their production on a country-by-country basis. The two strongest producers (Britain refused to participate) would thereafter co-operate and not compete with each other, and the revival of the Ruhr would no longer be a threat to France.

However, the French were not prepared to agree to Germany's remilitarisation without a struggle, and certainly not on the comparatively liberal terms proposed by the United States. Since the elite of the French army was fighting in Indochina, the French could not view with equanimity the revival of German military power. They refused to yield even when Truman threatened to abandon promised American financial and military aid to NATO if France persisted with her objections.

In October 1950 the French put forward the Pleven Plan for a European Defence Community – a scheme for a European army composed of France, West Germany, Italy, Belgium, Holland and Luxembourg, to which each member would contribute military units. This army would be under a supra-national European military organisation, with its own European Minister of Defence. As such it was designed to prevent the rise of a separate West German national army. Instead, German contingents would be closely tied to West European defence. The United States accepted this proposal in December 1950, although few military experts had much faith in the military effectiveness of such an organisation, and Britain refused to participate.

The French convened a European Army Conference on 15 February 1951 – the negotiations were to be long drawn out and contentious – and meanwhile the United States provided Western Europe with the additional troops and financial assistance she had earlier threatened to withhold. General Dwight D. Eisenhower, the wartime Supreme Commander of the Allied Expeditionary Forces in Europe, was appointed to the post of Supreme Commander of NATO on 19 December 1950 and the Supreme Headquarters of the Allied Powers in Europe (SHAPE) formally assumed its full functions at the Astoria Hotel in Paris on 2 April 1951 [23].

(vii) Conclusion

In 1945 the United States hoped to co-operate with the Soviet Union to maintain world peace and to promote world economic recovery. Similarly, Stalin had no wish to become involved in a renewed conflict, this time with the United States, and he believed that Soviet interests in the post-war world could be safeguarded by collaboration with America. President Truman did not altogether share the suspicions of Winston Churchill or some of his own advisers about the Soviet Union. Not that Churchill wanted a quarrel with the Soviet Union either: he wanted the West to adopt a policy of firmness towards the Russians which, he believed, would lead Stalin to co-operate with the West in a spirit of compromise. Subsequently Truman adopted a policy of firmness but this served merely to increase Stalin's already burgeoning suspicions of the United States.

It was the steady stream of Soviet actions in Eastern and Central Europe, in Germany, in the Eastern Mediterranean and in Iran which aroused Truman's fears about her ultimate ambitions. Individually these actions might have been passed off as Soviet efforts to safeguard her security, as in her demands for a change in the Straits regime in her favour, or her economic interests, as in the case of her pressure for oil concessions in North Iran, but collectively they appeared to the West as a deliberate programme designed to undermine Western influence in areas bordering the Soviet Union as a prelude to a complete communist take-over of these lands.

The transformation of the attitude of the United States administration and of large sections of the Senate from one of cautious optimism in the summer of 1945 about the prospects for American-Soviet co-operation, to one of implacable hostility towards Soviet designs, was not finally accomplished until 1947. However, evidence that the climate of opinion in offical circles in Washington was already turning against the Soviet Union in February 1946 (and of course some officials had long held suspicions of Soviet policy) was provided by the receptivity with which the State Department greeted the famous 'long telegram' of 8000 words sent by George F. Kennan, the United States Chargé d'Affaires in Moscow, to Byrnes on the 22nd, in answer to a query by the Secretary of State about the direction of Soviet foreign policy. This telegram was widely circulated within the Washington bureaucracy and was to provide the intellectual basis for the doctrine of 'containment' by which the United States attempted to prevent further Soviet encroachments beyond the areas they had occupied in 1945 [36].

Kennan wrote that the combination of Russian nationalism, Marxism, the historical Russian distrust of the outside world and their sense of insecurity and inferiority *vis-à-vis* the West, made the Soviet threat to the United States a particularly dangerous one. In these circumstances there could not, in the foreseeable future, be a permanent resolution of the United States differences with the Soviet Union, which would continue with her efforts both to undermine the West and to expand into regions at present outside her control. Only by a determined, patient, firm and long-term policy of resistance could the United States thwart Soviet ambitions.

This gloomy prognosis was seized on avidly in Washington both as an explanation for Soviet malevolence and as a justification for increased American vigilance. Nevertheless this official hostility towards the Soviet Union did not permeate American public opinion completely until 1947 – there still remained the possibility for a compromise between the two powers. Stalin was not anxious to risk a complete breach with the Western powers until the Marshall Plan convinced him that the United States was seeking to use her financial strength to bring Western Europe completely under her influence. The readiness of Czechoslovakia and Poland to accept American aid under the plan led Moscow to fear that the United States was also challenging Soviet control over Central and Eastern Europe [25].

The Berlin blockade in 1948 – a Soviet attempt to prevent the creation of a separate West Germany tied to the West – persuaded Truman that war might break out as a result of Soviet miscalculation of United States resolve to defend her interests in Europe. His firmness over West Berlin and United States participation in NATO in 1949 seemed to convince Moscow that Western security in Europe could not be compromised. Thereafter, until the late 1950s, the Soviet Union made no further overt moves in Europe.

The North Korean invasion of South Korea in June 1950, following Mao Tse-tung's victory in China in 1949 and the Soviet explosion of the atomic bomb in the same year, were regarded as further blows to American security. They resulted in the 'militarisation' of the Cold War. American expenditure on armaments of all kinds shot up from the comparatively low levels of the late 1940s. The armed forces of both the United States and the Soviet Union were now fully equipped for all-out war, while the number of nuclear weapons in the arsenals of each country multiplied. The insults which each side levelled at the other in diplomatic exchanges as well as through propaganda organs were couched more in the language of adversaries at war than of peaceful members of the international community [25; 63].

The United States now found herself involved in a military conflict for the first time since 1945, and in Asia, an area where she had least expected trouble to arise. The intervention of communist China in the Korean War in November 1950 convinced Truman that the war had been engineered by Moscow as a means of distracting United States attention from Europe. American forces in both Europe and Korea were strengthened. The Cold War reached a new peak of tension in 1950 and 1951 with the United States feverishly rearming and Soviet-American relations more embittered than ever.

Truman faced considerable pressure from the pro-Chiang Kai-shek (mostly the Republican 'Asia First') lobby in the United States, and from General MacArthur in Japan, to use Chiang Kai-shek's forces and American air power to smash the communist regime in China. Truman was determined to keep the Korean War limited to the peninsula: its extension to China, he believed, would lead to Soviet intervention and nuclear holocaust. As a result, after the spring of 1951, the Korean War became stalemated along the 38th parallel. American frustration with this situation – the first war in modern American military experience where outright victory could not be achieved – boiled over into a relentless search for scapegoats, inside and outside the administration, who could be held responsible for America's successive foreign policy failures since 1949. This anti-communist crusade poisoned American politics in the late 1940s and the 1950s and made it extremely difficult for successive administrations to formulate a coherent foreign policy [56].

3   The Cold War Continues, 1953–1960

(i) Eisenhower becomes President, 1953

The victory of Dwight D. Eisenhower, Supreme Commander in Europe during the Second World War, Army Chief of Staff after 1945 and latterly Supreme Commander of NATO, in the November 1952 presidential election – the first Republican to enter the White House since Herbert Hoover in 1929 – was partly attributable to the mounting frustration of the electorate with Truman's seeming inability to end the long drawn out and inconclusive stalemate in Korea. Armistice talks between the communist and United Nations military commands had begun in the summer of 1951, but progress had been painfully slow, and in 1952 had come to an end altogether when the two sides had been unable to reach agreement on the question of the repatriation of prisoners of war. The communists insisted on their forcible repatriation, while the Americans, for humanitarian reasons and also because they sensed a propaganda victory if large numbers of communist prisoners refused to return to their homelands, demanded voluntary repatriation. Eisenhower had anchored his presidential campaign on a pledge to end the Korean War quickly if elected [44].

Recent writers on Eisenhower's presidency have tried to restore his reputation which suffered, during the 1960s, from invidious comparisons with his dynamic successor, John F. Kennedy. Eisenhower was then portrayed as an ineffectual leader who preferred golf to affairs of state, leaving much of the decision-making to his subordinates. In recent years this view has been modified significantly. The relative prosperity of the 1950s has been compared favourably with the traumas of external and internal conflict which engulfed the United States in the succeeding two decades. Eisenhower is now represented by many writers as a skilful politician who kept a firm, if discreet, control over the actions of his military and civilian advisers, who insisted on deep cuts in defence expenditures (and resisted all pressures to restore them later) and opposed costly interventions by American land forces in overseas conflicts. Although the President was as suspicious of communist aims as his hard-line Secretary of State, John Foster Dulles, Eisenhower was more flexible, willing to overrule Dulles and seize opportunities to relax East–West tension, even if he remained convinced that the fundamental antagonism between the two sides was too deep to permit a genuine *rapprochement* [6; 18]. A rather more critical biographer, Piers Brendon, described Eisenhower in his recent book as a true representative of the 'middle class, middle brow, middle-of-the-road Middle America' [11:7], conservative and anti-communist, yet not fanatically so, an archetypal American of the 1950s.

During the early years of his presidency Eisenhower was inhibited from taking advantage of Soviet approaches to Washington for a relaxation of tension after Stalin's death in March 1953 by a vicious anti-communist crusade led by Senator Joseph McCarthy of Wisconsin. McCarthy began to exploit the growing fear of domestic communism in 1950 as a means of reviving his flagging political fortunes. It succeeded beyond his wildest dreams. Assisted by the spread of television across America, McCarthy soon became a national figure. For a few years, until he was finally discredited in 1954, he hounded hundreds of alleged communists in public life through the Senate Committee on Government Operations, of which he was chairman. Many of them were innocent: all their careers were destroyed. His activities spread fear throughout American society: even Eisenhower, who privately abhorred him, was reluctant to speak out against him – 'I will not get in the gutter with that guy' – and left it to others to bring about the Senator's downfall [6:*141*].

Stalin's successor, G.M. Malenkov, sought to emphasise consumer production at the expense of both heavy industry and the Soviet armed forces. This alteration in domestic priorities would require greater contacts with the West: the Soviet Union would need access to United States technological expertise if her domestic economy was to be transformed. In his speeches, Malenkov insisted that an armed clash between communism and capitalism would be suicidal in the nuclear age. While communism would ultimately triumph, this would be accomplished by peaceful means, and meanwhile the two camps should discuss ways of reducing tension. Given the hysterical anti-communist atmosphere in the United States, Eisenhower and Dulles ignored these Soviet feelers, arguing that a real reconciliation between the two sides could only come about if the Soviet Union rejected communism and embraced true democracy.

There is, however, evidence that the new Kremlin rulers did encourage Mao Tse-tung to adopt a more flexible approach to the Korean truce talks. They wanted to end a potentially dangerous source of East–West confrontation. Mao sought to remove his forces from North Korea and concentrate on the reconstruction of China. Rumours that Eisenhower contemplated air strikes on the Chinese mainland, including the use of nuclear weapons, may also have persuaded the Chinese to give way over the prisoners-of-war question and to agree to voluntary repatriation. The Korean armistice was signed on 27 July 1953 on the basis of the division of Korea at the 38th parallel: all subsequent attempts at unification foundered on the intense suspicions between the two Koreas [44].

(ii) 'The New Look' defence policy

The ending of the fighting in Korea enabled Eisenhower to fulfil Republican campaign promises that defence expenditure would be significantly reduced. His 'New Look' defence policy was based on increased reliance on the deterrent effect of nuclear weapons – hydrogen as well as atomic (the United States had test exploded a hydrogen bomb in November 1952) – enabling the United States to reduce the size of her conventional forces. Countries facing a communist threat would in future have to rely on their own forces for their defence, backed up by the threat of American nuclear support. In Western Europe NATO would rely more on small 'tactical nuclear weapons' and 'trip wire' conventional forces, thus saving US manpower, although this enabled the West Europeans to go back their earlier promises to expand their conventional forces. Britain, who was to explode her own atomic bomb, followed the American example in 1957 by announcing that she too would rely in future on her independent nuclear deterrent rather than upon large conscripted conventional forces [39; 46].

This American reliance on the threat of massive nuclear retaliation in the event of aggression was much criticised inside the United States, not only by army and navy leaders angry about ensuing reductions in manpower and ships, but also by a new group of civilian defence analysts, working in various privately funded (often by the defence industries) foundations. These critics denounced the 'New Look' as a dangerous gamble likely to force the United States in the event of a crisis to choose between a humiliating climb down or the unleashing of a mutually devastating nuclear exchange with the Soviet Union. They demanded that the United States maintain sufficient conventional strength to enable her to intervene in land conflicts where the threat of nuclear war was inappropriate [51]. Neither Eisenhower nor Dulles paid much attention to these attacks on the 'New Look', believing that the fear of an American nuclear response would discourage the communists from initiating adventures such as the Korean War. Dulles felt that verbal demonstrations of anti-communist pugnacity and a willingness to go to the brink of war in the event of any communist challenge to the West would be sufficient to force the communists to back down [33]. Eisenhower had no intention of reversing his reductions in American non-nuclear military capabilities. He feared that an overemphasis on military preparedness would unbalance the American economy and ultimately menace American society and its values. He was profoundly suspicious of what he later described as 'the military-industrial complex' which, if it grew too powerful, would be able to dictate American domestic and foreign policy and turn the United States into a 'garrison state'. The United States should remain calm in the face of communist provocations and concentrate on maintaining a stable and credible defence posture [6].

(iii) Dien Bien Phu and the Geneva Conference, 1954

The first major challenge to Eisenhower's policy, and one which demonstrated his cautious attitude, arose over Indochina in 1954. Despite American material assistance, which amounted to about 70 per cent of the costs of the French military effort, by 1954 the French army was losing its long struggle to subdue Ho Chi Minh's Vietminh forces. In March, when a French army corps, besieged by the Vietminh in the north-western garrison of Dien Bien Phu, faced imminent defeat, the French government appealed to the United States for military intervention as the only way of saving its army from annihilation. As a first step France requested the United States air force to bomb Vietminh positions around Dien Bien Phu. Dulles and Admiral Arthur W. Radford, the chairman of the United State Joint Chiefs of Staff, favoured the idea but the Army Chief of Staff, General Matthew Ridgway, feared that if the air strikes failed the United States would be forced to send in ground forces and that China might then intervene and the United States be faced with another long and bloody war. Eisenhower agreed with Ridgway: moreover France had hardly helped her own cause by refusing, despite American pressure, to grant real independence to her former possessions in Indochina. However, Dulles informed the French that the United States would deploy her air power if America's allies, and particularly Britain, would agree to commit forces to the fighting. Senate approval for American air action would also be essential. Eisenhower was well aware that Britain, with heavy overseas commitments and inadequate resources, would never agree to contribute troops to help the French. At the same time Congressional leaders were opposed, as the President had anticipated, to American intervention in Indochina. Eisenhower therefore refused the French request. It seems clear that the President was opposed to assisting the French in what might become a second Korean-type war. To avoid American intervention he took refuge in a typical ploy which enabled him to blame Britain and other allies of the United States for his failure to help France [6].

The French government, faced with defeat in Indochina, decided to negotiate an end to the war and, at the end of April 1954, an international conference of the powers concerned with the Far East, including communist China, opened in Geneva to discuss the future of Korea and Indochina, although no agreement could be reached on the former country which remained divided at the 38th parallel. The French army at Dien Bien Phu was forced to surrender on 7 May. This humiliation did not, however, prevent an eventual settlement of the conflict on terms which were not unfavourable to the West. The Soviet Union and communist China, anxious to end a conflict which might lead to a new East–West confrontation, pressed Ho Chi Minh to make concessions. The Vietminh and France agreed to an armistice in Indochina with a temporary partition of Vietnam along the 17th parallel. The Vietminh were to control the North and the French army the South until elections in 1956 resulted in the unification of the country, when the French would withdraw. The United States and South Vietnam refused to recognise this agreement. The United States began to supply arms and military advisers to a new South Vietnamese government controlled by an anti-communist American protégé, Ngo Dinh Diem. The French withdrew their troops in April 1956. Supported by the United States, Diem refused to agree to the holding of the all-Vietnam elections in 1956 which he suspected would result in a communist victory. Gradually the two Vietnams developed separately, with Ho Chi Minh strengthening his hold on the North and Diem, backed by the Unted States, consolidating his position in the South [5].

(iv) The advent of Khrushchev

In February 1955 Malenkov was ousted from the Soviet leadership by his rival, the Party Secretary Nikita Khrushchev, and by Marshal Bulganin, the former Defence Minister, who became Prime Minister. Ebullient, temperamental and outspoken, Khrushchev, allied to party hard liners like the Foreign Minister, Molotov, the Red Army generals and leaders of heavy industry, bitterly attacked Malenkov's consumerism and his willingness to treat the capitalist West as no longer a military threat to the Soviet Union. However, once in power, Khrushchev broke with his erstwhile allies and adopted many of Malenkov's policies, calling for increased production of consumer goods, the reform and expansion of agriculture, and reductions in the size of the Red Army (which fell from 5.8 million men to 3.6 million by 1960 – Stalin had increased its size in the late 1940s). He also demanded a more liberal approach to the satellite states, a Soviet reconciliation with Tito, peaceful co-existence with the West and the accomplishment of communist goals by peaceful means.

In a major speech to a secret session of the Twentieth Party Congress in February 1956, Khrushchev denounced the evils and excesses of Stalin's rule and by implication condemned his opponents in the Communist Party, such as Molotov, who had been closely associated with Stalin during the purges. His speech, however, stopped short of a root and branch condemnation of Stalinism – Khrushchev had also been close to Stalin, while many of his moderate supporters in the party opposed a witch hunt against the hard liners. In May 1955 he had inaugurated a relaxation in European tension by agreeing to Allied evacuation from, and the neutralisation of, Austria, by withdrawing Soviet troops from occupied Finnish territory and by meeting Eisenhower and the French and British prime ministers at Geneva in July 1955 which, despite the failure of arms control proposals, led to a significant, if temporary, improvement in East–West relations.

However, Khrushchev's willingness to talk to the West contributed to the growing divergence between the Soviet

Union and communist China since Stalin's death. Mao bitterly resented Khrushchev's attacks on Stalin and the 'cult of the personality' (Stalin's) in the Soviet Union – after all the Chinese Communist Party had built up Mao as a charismatic leader – and Khrushchev had delivered his speech without any advance consultation with Peking. He claimed that Khrushchev's departure from Stalinist orthodoxy would encourage separatist tendencies throughout the communist world. While Khrushchev made repeated efforts to improve relations with Peking after 1955, the divisions between them grew worse in the late 1950s. Mao feared that improved Soviet-American relations could only be achieved at the expense of Chinese interests. In 1960 Khrushchev withdrew 12,000 Soviet technical advisers from China, who were working on China's programme of modernisation. He also refused to supply China with nuclear information which had been promised earlier. The breach became complete during the 1960s when serious border disputes arose between the two powers: China claimed large areas of the Asiatic Soviet Union as her territory and large-scale clashes resulted which could have triggered a Sino-Soviet war [43].

Khrushchev's policy led to a relaxation of the Soviet grip on the East European satellites, where many of Stalin's appointees were replaced by more moderate communists. He also embarked on an active policy of trying to wean the emerging non-communist countries of the Third World away from United States influence by offering them Soviet aid and moral support, embarking on well publicised visits to India, Burma and Afghanistan. This policy not only upset the Chinese but, when applied to the Middle East, angered London and Washington. In 1955 Czechoslovakia began to supply arms to Egypt – hitherto Britain and the United States had monopolised arms sales to the Arab States and Israel, and had attempted to maintain the military balance between them by rationing their arms deliveries. When the United States refused an Egyptian request for additional arms, Egypt turned to the Soviet bloc. While Dulles recognised the dangers implicit in Khrushchev's efforts to ally Soviet Communism with the forces of Third World nationalism, he was unable to devise a satisfactory policy to counter the

67

threat. He failed to recognise (as indeed did the Soviet Union) that Third World nationalists would react just as sharply to Soviet interference in their internal affairs as they had to similar Western attempts.

A group of Asian and African countries, led by India, rejected alignment with either bloc, but Dulles tended to equate 'neutralism' (or 'non-alignment' as it was called) with pro-communism. His answer to communist expansionism was to complete the policy, begun by the Truman administration, of forming a network of alliances in Asia and the Middle East. After 1951 the United States entered into security pacts with the Philippines, South Korea, Formosa, Japan, Australia and New Zealand. In September 1954 she set up the South East Asia Treaty Organisation (SEATO) with France, the United Kingdom, Australia, New Zealand, Thailand, the Philippines and Pakistan, providing for joint action against aggression, and whose provisions were extended to South Vietnam. In the Middle East, the setting up, with American blessing although not with her active participation, of the Central Treaty Organisation or Baghdad Pact, consisting of Britain, Turkey, Iraq, Iran and Pakistan, increased Egyptian suspicions of British policy in the area – the governments of the member countries tended to be pro-British and anti-Egyptian [33].

(v) The Suez Crisis 1956

Egypt had been under the control of a group of nationalist army officers led by Colonel Abdul Gamel Nasser since 1952. Nasser was dedicated to eradicating Western influence from Egypt and eventually from the entire Middle East. In 1954 he achieved what had eluded his predecessors when Britain agreed to evacuate her troops from the Suez Canal zone, which they had occupied since 1881. Since the evacuation, however, Anglo-Egyptian relations had deteriorated significantly. The British Prime Minister, Anthony Eden, suspected that Nasser entertained ambitions to dominate the Middle East by destroying Britain's waning hegemony in the area. Eden saw the hand of Moscow behind Nasser's alleged intrigues against the pro-British rulers of Jordan and Iraq, and was also concerned about the security of Britain's vital oil supplies through the Suez Canal. In a final effort to win Nasser's good will, the United States and Britain promised him a large loan in December 1955 to finance a major Egyptian irrigation and power project, the Aswan Dam on the Lower Nile. However, Nasser's continued flirtation with the Soviet Union, his anti-British propaganda in the Middle East and his formation, in April 1956, of an alliance against Israel with Saudi Arabia, Syria and the Yemen so incensed Dulles and Eden that on 26 July 1956 they withdrew the promised loan. In retaliation, and as a means of financing the Aswan Dam, Nasser then nationalised the British and French-owned Suez Canal Company. To Eden this was the last straw. Unless Nasser was punished his influence would triumph throughout the Middle East. While Dulles tried to seek a compromise by setting up a committee of canal users to manage the canal and to secure compensation for the company from Egypt, the British Prime Minister entered into secret negotiations with France and Israel to find more forceful means of dealing with the Egyptian leader. Britain agreed to join France and Israel in a tripartite invasion of Egypt in the hope that the humiliation of Nasser would lead to his overthrow and replacement by more moderate Egyptians willing to adopt pro-British policies. France wanted to stop the flow of Egyptian arms to the Algerian nationalists, who were in open rebellion against their French rulers. Israel, facing the exclusion of her shipping from an Egyptian-owned Suez Canal, apprehensive that Nasser was seeking the leadership of the Middle East in a crusade against Israel, and angered by Egyptian-backed terrorist outrages across the Sinai desert, agreed to provide the French and British with a pretext for intervention by invading the Suez Canal. Britain and France would then call on both sides to withdraw from the Canal zone and at the same time send an Anglo-French force to occupy the area.

In the event, however, the Anglo-French plan badly miscarried. While the Israelis launched a successful attack on Egyptian army positions on 29 October and seized the Sinai Desert, the Anglo-French forces took several days to reach Alexandria (on 4 November). The delay enabled world opinion and the United States, alike outraged by what they regarded as a flagrant act of imperialist agression, to mobilise opposition to the Anglo-French invasion. Neither Britain nor France had taken the United States fully into their confidence about their plans, hoping that Washington would accept their *fait accompli* without much protest. Eisenhower had no intention of supporting this reckless act which would brand the United States as a fellow colonialist and would enable Moscow to pose as the sole protector of Arab nationalism.

While Khrushchev proposed to send Russian 'volunteers' to help Egypt and blustered that the Soviet Union would shower Britain and France with rockets if they did not withdraw, the United States rejected a Soviet call for joint Soviet-American action against Britain and France. Instead the United States sponsored a United Nations resolution calling for the removal of Anglo-French troops and their replacement by a United Nations peace-keeping force. Britain, virtually isolated and facing American financial and oil sanctions (Nasser had blocked the Suez Canal) called off the invasion. Anglo-French troops were evacuated from Egypt on 22 December 1956. The outcome was a triumph for Nasser, despite the poor showing of his army during the invasion, and a bitter blow to British prestige. Her position in the Middle East never fully recovered from this debacle [5; 33].

Ill health and the consequences of his miscalculations over Suez forced Eden to resign as Prime Minister in January 1957. He was replaced by Harold Macmillan, whose skilful diplomacy soon enabled Britain to restore close relations with the United States. This process was assisted by Nasser's failure to co-operate with the United States in the Middle East despite her support for Egypt during the Suez crisis. Indeed, Nasser's increased post-Suez prestige in the Arab world tempted him to further his ambitions in the area. Radio Cairo intensified its anti-Western propaganda throughout the Middle East. Early in 1957 an anti-Western left-wing government came to power in Syria, a result, the United States suspected, of Nasserite machinations (in January 1958 Egypt and Syria merged to form the short-lived United Arab

Republic). These developments prompted Eisenhower in January 1957 to secure from Congress authority to provide economic and military assistance to any Middle East country threatened by armed aggression or internal subversion (the so-called 'Eisenhower Doctrine'). In July 1958 the pro-British King of Iraq and his Prime Minister were murdered by pro-Nasserite Iraqi army officers who thereupon withdrew Iraq from the Central Treaty Organisation. When internal unrest, which Washington claimed was inspired by Nasser's agents, spread to the Lebanon and Jordan and threatened the stability of the pro-Western governments there, Eisenhower invoked his Doctrine and sent American troops to the Lebanon. Macmillan despatched a British force to Jordan. The regimes in these two countries survived [5].

(vi) The Hungarian uprising, 1956

The Anglo-French invasion of the Suez Canal enabled the Soviet Union to proclaim her solidarity with the aspirations of Arab nationalism. It also distracted world attention from the Soviet invasion of Hungary in November 1956. Khrushchev's denunciation of Stalin's excesses and his support from a degree of political and economic liberalisation in the satellites had unleashed a wave of reformism in Poland and the other Central and East European countries. The ferment reached uncontrollable proportions in Hungary, where a popular revolt against its Stalinist rulers in October led to the setting up of a new government under Imry Nagy which, on 1 November 1956, announced Hungary's virtual withdrawal from the Soviet bloc.

This was too much for the Kremlin and, on 4 and 5 November 1956, Soviet troops and tanks moved into the capital, Budapest, and Nagy was deposed and arrested (he was later shot). He was replaced as Prime Minister by Janos Kadar, a pro-Soviet communist. American radio propaganda from Western Europe and Dulles's rhetoric about the need to 'roll back' the Soviet frontiers had deluded the Hungarians into the belief that the United States would support their revolt, but neither Eisenhower nor Dulles was willing to provoke a nuclear war by intervening in what they accepted as a Soviet sphere of influence. The result of the Hungarian uprising was a flood of Hungarian refugees to the West and frequent American-inspired United Nations resolutions calling on the Soviet Union to withdraw her forces from Hungary. Inevitably these gestures had not the slightest effect on the Soviet Union and the episode merely exposed the hollowness of 'roll-back' to any satellites who might seek to emulate the Hungarian example [49].

Indeed, the Hungarian uprising seemed to confirm Peking's criticisms of Khrushchev's policy. Dulles was not unaware of the growing rift between Peking and Moscow but he believed that, if he responded to Chinese hints that improved relations between China and the United States were possible, China would use this to play off the United States against the Soviet Union. His suspicions of Peking's ambitions were increased when in 1954 communist China declared her intention of 'liberating' nationalist-held Formosa in the near future. This was followed by heavy Chinese artillery bombardments in 1954 and early 1955 of the two nationalist-occupied islands of Quemoy and Matsu. These were repeated in 1958. Fearing an imminent Chinese invasion, Eisenhower warned China that the United States would help the nationalists to defend the islands, signed an alliance with Chiang Kai-shek late in 1954, and sent American destroyers to escort Chiang's troop reinforcements to Quemoy in the autumn of 1958. This example of American 'brinkmanship' appeared to deter China from taking any further action [6].

(vii) The missile gap

Khrushchev also exhibited an increasing tendency to threaten a Soviet nuclear attack on the West during periods of tension (the Suez crisis was one example of this). In 1953 the Soviet Union tested a hydrogen bomb and in August 1957 she launched an Intercontinental Ballistic Missile (ICBM) before the United States. Then on 4 October 1957, in a blaze of publicity, the Soviet Union successfully launched the world's first man-made space satellite, Sputnik I: the United

States was still experimenting with a prototype. These demonstrations of Soviet technological expertise were bitter blows to United States pride and to her confidence in her prowess in this field. There ensued inside the United States a vigorous Congressional and press campaign, supported by air force chiefs and the aerospace industry, calling for a priority American missile and space programme. Eisenhower's critics claimed that his preoccupation with defence economies had enabled the Soviet Union to overtake the United States in an area vital to her defence and security. The critics charged that the complacent and penny-pinching Eisenhower administration had allowed the Soviet Union to win a technological victory over the United States in an area in which Americans had always prided themselves on their superiority. Democratic politicans, such as Senators John F. Kennedy of Massachusetts and Lyndon B. Johnson of Texas, seized on the issue to further their chances in the race for the Democratic presidential nomination in 1960. American service chiefs were only too willing to supply them with confidential and exaggerated information about the poor state of American defences, calculating, wrongly as it turned out, that the ensuing political pressure would force the President to increase defence expenditure.

Eisenhower refused to embark on a major arms race, although he did authorise a slight increase in missile research and development. He steadfastly rejected demands for increases in bomber production or in conventional military capabilities. Since 1956 secret flights over Soviet territory by United States U-2 photographic reconnaissance planes had provided the President with evidence which suggested that Khrushchev's claims that the Soviet Union was constructing a large number of ICBMs were fraudulent: that the Soviet Union lacked the manufacturing capacity for this. However, the sensitive nature of these surveillance operations made it impossible for the administration to refute the alarmist figures brandished by its domestic critics about the so-called missile gap: the belief that by the early 1960s the Soviet Union would have an assured superiority in nuclear weapons and delivery systems over the United States. That in fact the reverse was true was not accepted publicly by the United States government until 1961 [3; 46].

(viii) The Berlin crisis and the Geneva Conference, 1958–1960

Khrushchev took advantage of the hysteria in the United States about the missile gap to try to achieve a diplomatic triumph over Berlin, from whence Stalin had failed to dislodge the West in 1948. The division of Germany into two separate republics was now virtually an accomplished fact and the problem of a West German contribution to NATO's defences had been resolved in May 1955. In August 1954 the French National Assembly had rejected the European Defence Community (EDC). However, Anthony Eden, then British Foreign Secretary, advanced a compromise proposal in September 1954 whereby West Germany contributed armed forces to NATO through the revival of the Brussels Pact, which was to be called the Western European Union (WEU), with the inclusion of West Germany and Italy. West Germany agreed not to manufacture nuclear and chemical weapons, missiles, bombers and warships. For her part Britain agreed to maintain on a permanent basis, and as a counter to a West German army, four army divisions and a tactical air force in West Germany. This offer helped the French to accept the plan by overcoming their fear that they might be left alone to face a resurgent West Germany. In 1955 the Federal Republic of (West) Germany joined NATO and was accepted as an equal partner in Western Europe [23]. The military division of Europe was confirmed in May 1955 by the formation of a Pact of Mutual Assistance and Unified Command (the Warsaw Pact), a military alliance based on mutual defence, consisting of the Soviet Union and the Central and Eastern European States, including the (East) German Democratic Republic (GDR), but not Yugoslavia.

Khrushchev was determined to end the anomalous position of West Berlin. While the Western sectors of that city remained under Allied military control and represented an island of prosperity in the centre of the relatively impoverished East Germany, the GDR might never become a stable ally of the Soviet Union. Large numbers of professional and skilled East Germans, whose services the hard-pressed East

German economy desperately needed, escaped to West Germany through Berlin. Khrushchev required a foreign policy success to strengthen his position inside the Soviet Union. In June 1957 his enemies in the party – Molotov, Lazar Kaganovitch and Malenkov – attempted to secure his dismissal at a meeting of the Party Presidium. Khrushchev outwitted them by calling for a full meeting of the Central Committee which, packed with his supporters, voted for the expulsion of Khrushchev's enemies from the Presidium. However, his opponents had been defeated but not vanquished. They remained party members and were eventually able to gain allies in the armed forces when the latter turned against Khrushchev's plan to reduce the size of Soviet ground forces and place more emphasis in the future on nuclear deterrence. Not until 1961 was Khrushchev able to manoeuvre the expulsion of the so-called 'anti-party' group (although many of them had already been exiled) from the party.

Thus, even after 1957, his position remained precarious. His decision to reduce further the number of active troops in the Red Army by 1.2 million men heightened his unpopularity in military circles. Mao Tse-tung came to the aid of his enemies by condemning his revisionist policies. In retaliation Khrushchev gave only lukewarm support to China during the Formosan crises and supplied India with aircraft during her border wars with China in the early 1960s [43].

In November 1958 Khrushchev announced that, unless the West agreed to negotiate the withdrawal of its troops from West Berlin within six months, the Soviet Union would sign a separate peace treaty with the German Democratic Republic and turn the West's access routes to West Germany over to East German officials. This placed the West in a dilemma: they would either be forced to deal with a regime they had promised West Germany in 1955 not to recognise, or they would be faced with a new confrontation over Berlin. Eisenhower could not abandon the West Berliners in the face of Khrushchev's threats – to have done so would have demonstrated to West Germany and to America's other allies that United States protection could not be relied upon. Khrushchev calculated that the United States would not risk nuclear war over Berlin. His conviction was strengthened when the United States and Britain hinted that they might be prepared to make some concessions. However, they made it clear that these would not include the withdrawal of their troops from the city, to Khrushchev the *sine qua non* of any agreement. The most he was prepared to concede was that Berlin should become a demilitarised city under the United Nations: once this had been achieved the Western Allies would withdraw, leaving West Berlin at the mercy of the GDR. However, after the Western powers agreed to hold a Foreign Ministers Conference in July 1959 in Geneva to discuss Germany and European security problems, Khrushchev, in February 1959, postponed his six months ultimatum. Then in a much publicised visit to the United States in September, Khrushchev mended his fences with Eisenhower, again suspended his Berlin deadline and agreed that the future of Berlin, the German question, and arms control should be discussed at a Big Four summit meeting in May 1960 [6].

Eisenhower did not believe that this summit would have any more success in resolving the German issue than previous great power meetings, but he hoped that it would at least lead to a further postponement of the Berlin issue and to a new relaxation of East–West tensions. The Americans were willing to conclude an agreement on the suspension of nuclear testing. Both the United States and the Soviet Union had recently concluded a massive series of tests and the heavy fall-out had excited widespread fears about the biological and other hazards which were being inflicted on human kind.

However, the conference collapsed almost as soon as it began: on 1 May the Soviets had shot down and captured intact a U-2 spy plane over their territory. In the ensuing fuss Eisenhower accepted full responsibility for the reconnaissance mission; he had, after all, authorised the flight. However, the President refused Khrushchev's demand for a full apology and the Soviet delegation thereupon walked out of the conference. The U-2 incident played into the hands of Khrushchev's Kremlin enemies who seized on it as evidence that the United States could not be trusted. Khrushchev cancelled an invitation to Eisenhower to visit the Soviet Union. Any hope for a recovery from the paralysis into which East–West relations had now been plunged would have to await the inauguration of a new American President in 1961 [5; 42].

(ix) Conclusion

In retrospect Eisenhower's presidency has been regarded as one of relative peace and prosperity in comparison with the experiences of his successors. In 1953 the armistice in Korea ended the hostilities there, although the division between North and South was unbridgeable. The anti-communist hysteria inside the United States subsided after 1954. Eisenhower managed to avoid active American involvement in foreign wars after 1953. His patience and firmness during periods of tension contrasted with the militancy of his Secretary of State, John Foster Dulles, who delivered frequent speeches about the evils of communism. While Eisenhower shared Dulles's intense anti-communism, he was the more flexible of the two and was not prepared to allow the Secretary of State a free hand in determining foreign policy. Dulles had been eager to send in the United States air force to assist the French at Dien Bien Phu and had been equally persistent in demanding the destruction of Chinese airfields on the mainland to forestall a Chinese assault on Quemoy and Matsu. He had also opposed Eisenhower's summit meeting with Bulganin and Khrushchev at Geneva in 1955, suspecting a Soviet manoeuvre to trick the West into lowering its guard. Eisenhower overruled his Secretary of State in all these cases – the United States did not assist the French by actively intervening in Indochina in 1954; the Quemoy and Matsu crises did not lead to war with China; and the President insisted on attending the Big Four Conference in Geneva in 1955, although the practical results were minimal [33].

Nevertheless the anti-communist climate in the administration and in Congress did inhibit Eisenhower from embarking on a far-reaching exploration of the possibility of reducing

American-Soviet tension after Stalin's death. In any case he shared many of their assumptions about the evils of communism. His dealings with the Soviet Union were dilatory and essentially negative. At Geneva the President put forward a dramatic proposal for the United States and the Soviet Union to open up each other's air space to aerial photography by each side – the so-called 'Open Skies' initiative. In Eisenhower's view this would be a confidence-building measure, looking forward to more concrete negotiations about arms control. When Khrushchev rejected the suggestion as a blatant American effort to engage in espionage operations over Soviet territory, Eisenhower dropped the matter and made no further suggestions. Even if the Paris summit of 1960 had not collapsed over the U-2 incident, it is doubtful whether it would have accomplished much in the area of arms control. The two superpowers had been discussing a possible test ban treaty in reaction to increasing international alarm about the dangers of nuclear fall-out from the stream of tests that were carried out in these years. While both the United States and the Soviet Union did eventually stop testing on a voluntary and temporary basis, there could be no permanent ban during a period of rapid technological change and experimentation, and while each side was competing with the other in missile development [17].

Despite Dulles's pre-election rhetoric in 1952, the nature of containment did not change much between 1949 and 1960. Eisenhower followed Truman in trying to apply the concept to Asia – an almost insuperable task given the political instability and intense nationalism which characterised the area. Acheson had applied the metaphor of a rotten apple in a barrel of apples which was likely to affect the rest in trying to convince Congress of the need to assist Greece and Turkey in 1947: on this analogy, if the two countries fell to communism, the rest of Europe and the Middle East would eventually follow [1]. Eisenhower followed Acheson's example on 7 April 1954 in discussing the dangers of Indochina falling to communism, although he applied the 'falling domino' analogy: 'You have a row of dominoes set up, you knock out the first one, and what will happen to the last one is the certainty that it will go over very quickly.' Thus, if

Indochina became communist-dominated, the contagion would spread to the rest of Asia [6:*180*].

Eisenhower's decision to provide military and financial aid to Diem's Republic of (South) Vietnam and to build up that country as an anti-communist bastion in Indochina, was to involve his successors in an expanding and dangerous commitment. His support for, and encouragement of, the subversion of allegedly anti-American regimes in the Middle East and Latin America by the Central Intelligence Agency, a policy espoused even more enthusiastically by subsequent incumbents of the White House, was to have unpleasant repercussions on America's international reputation and on her internal constitutional processes when it was revealed later. The plan to use Cuban refugees to invade Cuba and overthrow the Castro regime was approved by Eisenhower. Yet, despite all this, Eisenhower's presidency saw communism firmly established in North Korea, North Vietnam and Cuba [11].

By 1960 there was a rising tide of dissatisfaction within the United States about the lacklustre performance of the Eisenhower presidency. The support which the President had so long enjoyed in Middle America fell away after 1957 as his administration became associated in the public mind with economic stagnation and defence and foreign policy failures. His increasing ill health also told against him. All this was bound to have an adverse effect on the election prospects of Richard M. Nixon, his Vice President, who was selected as the Republican presidential candidate in 1960. By contrast, John F. Kennedy, the Democratic presidential candidate, was to appeal to many Americans as a man who would revive America's prestige in the world after the setbacks the United States had suffered during the Eisenhower years. Kennedy promised to revitalise the flagging American economy, devote more resources to defence expenditure, reinvigorate America's demoralised allies and embark on an active policy of countering communism in the Third World by a vigorous assertion of American values and by liberal, yet responsible, injections of American aid [7; 18; 53].

4 Kennedy, Khrushchev and the Decline of the Cold War

(i) Kennedy becomes President

As Democratic candidate for the presidency in 1960 Kennedy had campaigned vigorously on the issue of American defence unpreparedness and on the dangers of the 'missile gap'. He had distanced himself from Eisenhower by stressing his youth and vigour (he was 43 in 1960: Eisenhower was nearly 70). He contrasted his bold programmes for a reinvigorated United States ('getting the United States moving again') with Eisenhower's feeble and lacklustre policies. Domestically this meant economic expansion and full employment, while in foreign policy terms his 'New Frontier' rhetoric insisted that in future the United States would ally herself with the progressive forces in the world. Nationalism would no longer, as in Dulles's day, be regarded as a potential threat to the free world – indeed, the United States would encourage and assist Third World aspirations. In his inaugural speech the new President declared that 'we shall pay any price, bear any burden, meet any hardship, support any friend, oppose any foe to assure the survival and success of liberty' [25:*205*]. This high-flown language presaged a more active policy, as universalist and anti-communist as Eisenhower's had been, but under Kennedy and Johnson, armed with sufficient military strength to enable the United States to act more decisively in situations where Eisenhower would probably have been more cautious [25].

Under Kennedy and his Defense Secretary, Robert McNamara, a statistical wizard who had been president of the Ford Motor Company, defence expenditure on both nuclear and conventional forces was dramatically increased. McNamara sought to rationalise and reform the American defence establishment and bring it more closely under the control of the Defense Department. The Democrats argued that an expanding American economy could afford to devote more resources to defence. Tight budget ceilings would be lifted although McNamara insisted that, by applying cost-benefit analysis methods, he would ensure that cost overruns on defence projects, the needless duplication of weapons systems and waste in the armed forces would be eliminated. The ensuing detailed and centralised scrutiny of all weapons procurement and development processes by civilian analysts based in McNamara's office angered the United States military chiefs, who complained that the system undermined their professional expertise and led to civilian interference in operational matters [35].

Nevertheless the joint chiefs of staff welcomed the expansion of their defence budgets which enabled them to increase the size of the United States army and navy. Expenditure on land- and sea-launched Intercontinental Ballistic Missiles (ICBMs) was also increased, but Kennedy soon discovered that the missile gap was a myth: not only did the United States have a superiority over the Soviet Union, but the Eisenhower administration had also developed more advanced solid-fuel-fired types which were quicker to fire and more accurate. This enabled McNamara to phase out some of the older first-generation liquid-fuelled missiles and to concentrate on the solid-fuelled Minuteman I and II ICBMs in hardened (heavily protected) silos and on the development of the relatively invulnerable Polaris submarine-launched missiles. By 1962 the United States possessed 250 land-based ICBMs, 144 Polaris missiles on 9 submarines and 630 B52 bombers. The Soviet Union had only 75 land-based ICBMs and 120 long-range bombers [3].

Kennedy had been privately informed by the Eisenhower administration during the 1960 election campaign that the missile gap did not exist, but continued to denounce the inadequate defence preparations of the Republicans: after all, the continuation of the missile gap myth was a strong card in his appeal to the voters and the fabrication fitted in with the perceptions of many Democratic voters about the feebleness of the previous administration. However, the knowledge of American missile superiority gave Kennedy greater confidence in dealing with Khrushchev's threats to sign a separate peace treaty with East Germany and was crucial to Kennedy's success in confronting the Soviet Union during the Cuban missile crisis in 1962.

(ii) The Bay of Pigs invasion

Kennedy's first venture into the military arena in 1961 was a disaster. In 1959 a Cuban nationalist, Fidel Castro, with a few supporters, had overthrown the dictator, Fulgencio Batista, in Cuba. Liberal Americans at first welcomed Castro, believing that he would establish a Western-style democracy in Cuba. They soon became disillusioned, however, when Castro set up a one-party state in close collaboration with the communists and began to encourage the spread of revolution elsewhere in Latin America. Business interests were also angered when he began to nationalise United States companies in Cuba. The United States retaliated by imposing economic and financial sanctions on Cuba and breaking off relations. Castro then turned to the Soviet Union for financial and military assistance. The Central Intelligence Agency (CIA), established in 1947 under the National Security Act to co-ordinate and collect information about potential enemies of the United States, had engaged in numerous covert activities overseas in the 1950s, including the overthrow of the anti-Western nationalist Prime Minister of Iran, Dr Muhammad Musaddiq, in 1953, and a coup which had overthrown President Arbenz of Guatemala in 1954. The CIA was already planning numerous measures to overthrow or assassinate Castro when Kennedy entered the White House in January 1961. One of the most promising of these was the arming and training of anti-Castro Cuban refugees in Florida in preparation for an invasion of Cuba. Kennedy, new to the presidency, and assured that the mission would be successful, authorised the invasion, although he insisted that there should be no direct involvement of American regular forces. The invasion was a fiasco: after landing on

82

the Bay of Pigs in Cuba on 14–15 April the American-backed anti-Castro forces were soon either killed or rounded up by Castro's troops. Kennedy's veto had prevented American air strikes which might have turned the tide in favour of the invaders. This was a major setback for Kennedy's prestige and may well have convinced Khrushchev that the youthful President was a bungling amateur [5].

(iii) The Vienna meeting, June 1961

On 2 and 4 June 1961 Kennedy met Khrushchev in Vienna. The meeting was not a success: Khrushchev threatened Kennedy with a new six-month ultimatum for ending the unsatisfactory status of West Berlin, and warned the new President that the USSR would continue supporting anti-Western guerrillas in the Third World. The only positive result of the meeting was an agreement on the establishment of a neutralist government in Laos, a country torn by civil war between American-supported right-wing forces and a communist-supported insurgent movement, the Pathet Lao. Neither the Soviet Union nor the United States was anxious for a major confrontation in Laos, a state crucial to the interests of neither. East–West tensions remained acute after the Vienna meeting as Khrushchev continued to threaten that he would turn the Berlin access routes over to the East Germans, and Kennedy insisted that the West would never abandon its rights in the city. In July 1961 Kennedy recalled the United States reserve forces to active duty and announced a 25 per cent increase in US military strength as a clear warning to the Soviet Union not to push the Berlin question too far. For the time being Khrushchev stayed his hand.

(iv) Vietnam

Meanwhile Kennedy was distracted by the deteriorating situation in South Vietnam. The new President continued Eisenhower's policy of supporting the Diem regime with military and financial assistance. However, after 1960 increasing communist guerrilla (Vietcong) activity in the south, backed by Ho Chi Minh in Northern Vietnam, led to the progressive demoralisation of the South Vietnamese army, and forced Kennedy to expand the US military mission in South Vietnam from 500 to 10,000 men and to authorise them to fight alongside the South Vietnamese army in the field. When Diem's autocratic rule provoked highly publicised acts of civil disorder among South Vietnam's Buddhist community, and rumours reached Washington that Diem was contemplating peace negotiations with the North, Kennedy authorised a CIA-backed South Vietnamese army coup against Diem, which took place on 1–2 November 1962. Diem and his brother were assassinated. This resulted only in increasing political instability in Saigon as contending military factions struggled for power. Kennedy fully accepted Eisenhower's assumption that the independence of South Vietnam was vital to United States security in South East Asia. He shared the previous administration's belief that if Saigon fell to Ho Chi Minh's Vietcong, the United States would not only have sustained a major defeat in the struggle with world communism but other countries in the area would lose faith in America's ability to defend them and would speedily succumb to communism. As a result the United States would face a communist-dominated Asia, and the virus might spread to Japan, which would be cut off from her markets and sources of food. However, Kennedy refused the advice of his military and civilian advisers that the United States should commit US regular forces to the support of the South Vietnamese army, which was sustaining defeat after defeat at the hands of the Vietcong. Nor would he agree to air strikes by the United States air force against North Vietnam. He feared that these steps would mark the beginning of a major United States military commitment to what might turn out to be a long drawn out and bloody struggle. The problem of Vietnam was a legacy Kennedy left to his successor, Lyndon B. Johnson, who was to have no scruples about sending the United States army and air force into South Vietnam, with all the consequences Kennedy had feared [5; 26; 56].

(v) The Cuban missile crisis

In the autumn and winter of 1962 Kennedy was facing a much more serious crisis nearer home. The Soviet Union had begun supplying Castro with military equipment and advisers in 1962, but stressed that this was a defensive measure. On 14 October 1962, however, American aerial reconnaissance over Cuba detected the presence of a launching pad and medium-range ballistic missiles, supervised by Soviet technicians. There is little doubt that this dangerous manoeuvre was Khrushchev's effort to secure the foreign policy success which had so far eluded him over Berlin, where Western determination to uphold the *status quo* had forced the Soviet leader to lift another six-months ultimatum he had issued to Kennedy in Vienna. He was facing continued opposition to his internal policy from the remaining hard-liners in the party, who were now joined by Red Army chiefs, who forced him to cancel the troop reductions he had announced in 1960 and to increase the Soviet military budget by one-third. A dramatic overseas success against the United States would enable Khrushchev to confront his internal critics and Peking, and rally the moderate forces in the party to resume the task of reform and *détente*.

The Kennedy administration had made it clear in September 1961 that it possessed a two-to-one superiority over the Soviet Union in ICBMs. The positioning of Soviet Medium Range Ballistic Missiles (MRBMs) in Cuba, capable of striking at targets inside the United States, would to some extent redress the nuclear balance in favour of the Soviet Union. Khrushchev was due to visit the United Nations General Assembly in New York in November 1962 and no doubt he intended to announce his Cuban missile coup in dramatic terms there as a prelude to demanding the withdrawal of Allied troops from Berlin. It was a typical Khrushchev move – an impulsive and risky action designed to take his enemies by surprise but one which could be justified by reference to the stationing of American MRBMs in Italy and Turkey, and by the need to defend Cuba against further American-supported invasions. Future arms limitation talks would also prove more meaningful if the USSR was in a position of near equality in missiles with the USA [57].

Khrushchev completely underestimated Kennedy's combative psychology. The President was bound to react vigorously, especially with mid-term Congressional elections due in November 1962. United States indignation was increased by repeated Soviet assurances to American diplomats that it would not place offensive weapons in Cuba. At the end of October Kennedy held frequent and exhausting meetings with his closest political and military advisers – McNamara, Dean Rusk (the Secretary of State), the joint chiefs of staff, his brother (Attorney General Robert Kennedy) and White House aides – to work out a response to the Soviet move. This committee considered a number of possibilities: to do nothing, which would be unthinkable both for political and diplomatic reasons; to use American troops to invade the island and destroy the missile sites, which would risk a nuclear confrontation with the Soviet Union; or to try to destroy the sites by surgical air attacks, which might equally result in such a confrontation, as Soviet technicians would be killed. The arguments ranged to and fro between the various options. Eventually Kennedy decided to adopt a more gradual, controlled response which would enable Khrushchev to back down without being totally humiliated.

In a television broadcast on 22 October Kennedy revealed to the American people the Soviet activities in Cuba, and warned the Soviet Union that 'any missile launched from Cuba against any nation in the Western hemisphere [would be regarded] as an attack by the Soviet Union on the United States requiring a full retaliatory response upon the Soviet Union' [42:228]. He announced that Cuba would be 'quarantined' by the United States navy: all vessels bound for the island would be stopped and searched and any found carrying missiles would be turned back. United States marines were massed in Florida, while Soviet diplomats in Washington were left in no doubt of Kennedy's determination to secure the removal of the missiles from Cuba. During the ensuing few days tension mounted as Moscow protested about the blockade and stated that, in accordance with international law, Soviet vessels would refuse to allow themselves to be searched. However, on Friday 26 October Khrushchev backed down. In a long and rambling letter to Kennedy he promised that the missile sites in Cuba would be closed down and the MRBMs returned to the Soviet Union if the USA would end the blockade and promise not to invade Cuba. Later that night, however, a second note arrived in Washington which adopted a more truculent tone, demanding that in return for the removal of Soviet missiles from Cuba, the United States should remove its missiles from Turkey. This note was no doubt inspired by Khrushchev's conservative critics in the Kremlin, who had from the outset entertained serious reservations about his Cuban escapade, and who now demanded that he should at least obtain some *quid pro quo* from the United States in order to salvage something from the wreckage. Kennedy, who refused to give any such undertaking (although he later ordered the removal of the obsolescent US missiles from Turkey), decided to ignore the contents of the second note. On 27 October, on instructions from Moscow, all Soviet ships carrying MRBM equipment for Cuba were turned back and the MRBM sites in Cuba were dismantled. The United States had won a decisive diplomatic triumph. The Berlin issue also died down as a major problem in East–West relations. The East Germans had erected a wall between East and West Berlin in August 1961 and this had effectively brought to an end the flow of refugees from the GDR to the West. The GDR now achieved a form of stability it had hitherto lacked [5; 37].

In retrospect the Cuban missile crisis led to the changed atmosphere in Soviet-American relations in 1963. Both sides had been shaken by the nearness of their approach to nuclear war in 1962. Khrushchev was now anxious for an improvement in relations with the United States. He was faced with a rising tide of criticism from within the Soviet hierarchy about his clumsy diplomacy which had resulted in a resounding blow to Soviet pride and prestige. Peking bitterly attacked his Cuban climb-down. Everything conspired against Khrushchev: even his bid for agricultural expansion in the Soviet Union resulted in spectacular harvest failures in 1963 [43].

In the United States the influence of high-level Pentagon and State Department officials, the service chiefs and key

Cabinet ministers on decision-making during the crisis was significant, although Kennedy had of course the final word. Truman and Eisenhower had kept the civilian and military bureaucracy at a distance and had tended to consult their subordinates only after they had made up their own minds about policy. Kennedy appeared to be more willing to listen to his officials' advice before making a decision. Moreover, while Eisenhower had been scrupulous in keeping Congressional leaders informed about developments, for instance during the crisis over Dien Bien Phu, Kennedy imparted only general information irregularly. Admittedly events during the Cuban crisis moved too fast to permit of close and frequent consultation between President and Congress, but nevertheless their role was relatively insignificant. If major hostilities had ensued there would have been no time for Congress to debate a declaration of war on the Soviet Union. Throughout, Kennedy relied on his power as Commander-in-Chief to determine military policy, a power which was to be employed more frequently by his successors.

(vi) The Test Ban Treaty, 1963

The collapse of the Paris summit in 1960 had put an end to discussions about a nuclear test ban treaty, although both the United States and the Soviet Union had ended testing for the time being. In September 1961, however, the Soviet Union resumed testing and the United States followed suit. The preliminary round of talks on the test ban question in the late 1950s had in any case been deadlocked by arguments about underground testing. Atmospheric testing could be detected easily by seismographic means, but not so underground tests, which could be confused with subterranean earthquakes. The United States had therefore insisted that an international inspectorate should be formed to monitor underground tests on site: the Soviet Union, which had always resisted what it regarded as a form of spying, at first demurred, although it later agreed to a limited number of inspections on its soil, but these were regarded as inadequate by the American side [17]. When, after the Cuban missile crisis, talks were resumed in Moscow between the United States, Britain and the Soviet Union in July 1963, the three powers signed a treaty banning testing in the atmosphere and under water, and by the late 1960s 100 nations had agreed to adhere to it.

At the same time the two countries agreed to establish a radio telephone link between the Kremlin and the White House – the so-called 'Hot Line' – to permit of immediate and direct consultations between the two leaders in the event of a crisis. No further progress, however, was made towards arms limitation.

(vii) The challenge of General de Gaulle

While tension between the Soviet Union and the United States receded in 1963, the United States was facing increasingly difficult relations with its main European ally, France. During the late 1950s economic and military collaboration between France and West Germany marked a major turning point in the relations between those historic enemies but, after 1956, France's relations with the United States began to deteriorate. France deeply resented the American economic and financial pressure which had caused Britain to withdraw so precipitately from the Suez imbroglio, dragging France with her. After her withdrawal from Indochina, France found herself faced with new upheavals in Algeria, where fighting had broken out between Algerian nationalists, who sought independence, and the French army. France had granted her other possessions in North Africa – Morocco and Tunisia – independence in 1955. She was determined, however, not to yield Algeria, which she regarded as part of France, and which contained a large number of French settlers, or *colons*, who were vociferous in their insistence that Algeria remain French.

American pressure on France to grant Algeria independence was bitterly resented in Paris and by the *colons*, while even more provoking to French pride were speeches by United States Senators, including John F. Kennedy, condemning French army excesses in Algeria. By 1958 the Fourth

Republic faced civil war as the *colons*, aided by sections of the French army, threatened to take over the central government. General Charles de Gaulle returned to power in France, dealt decisively with the insurrectionists, and gradually withdrew the French army from Algeria, which became independent in 1961. de Gaulle had meanwhile established the Fifth Republic which, for the first time since 1851, gave the presidency, which de Gaulle occupied, considerable powers over internal and external policy.

de Gaulle was determined to restore France's international standing. In 1961 France tested an atomic bomb, the basis for her independent deterrent, the *force de frappe*. de Gaulle had already, in 1958, challenged American domination of NATO, demanding that the United States, France and Britain set up a three-power directorate to run the organisation – a demand rejected by the United States as likely to alienate the other members of NATO. de Gaulle also doubted that the United States would risk her own destruction by employing her nuclear arsenal in the event of a Soviet attack on Europe. Periodic debates in Congress over the need to retain expensive United States ground troops in Germany increased French doubts about American reliability. de Gaulle called for genuine sharing of nuclear decision-making between Britain, France and the United States instead of American monopolisation of that weapon; a demand Washington also rejected [28].

de Gaulle bitterly attacked Britain's role in Europe. After Suez Britain seemed to the French to be drifting more and more into the role of a Washington satellite, suspicions which were increased by the close nuclear relationship between Britain and the United States. During the late 1950s Britain had embarked on the development of her own intermediate ballistic missile, Blue Streak, but in 1960 she had abandoned it in favour of purchasing a more advanced American model, Skybolt. This would, she hoped, enable her to keep her ageing fleet of long-range V-bombers operational down to 1970. In 1962, as part of his standardisation programme, McNamara had cancelled the production of Skybolt in favour of developing the more effective and more easily concealed submarine-launched missile, the Polaris. Anxious to end nuclear proliferations which would complicate future arms limitation negotiations, McNamara was at first unwilling to provide Britain with a replacement for Skybolt, but then Macmillan appealed to Kennedy on the issue. At a meeting with the British Prime Minister at Nassau in the Bahamas in December 1962 Kennedy agreed that the British should be supplied with three Polaris submarines [9]. France received a similar offer which de Gaulle rejected.

The United States sought to satisfy European aspirations for some say in nuclear weapons by setting up in March 1963 a multilateral fleet (MLF) of twenty-five surface ships carrying Polaris missiles, which would be manned by sailors from several NATO countries. This led to anxious enquiries by Moscow as to whether the MLF would give West Germany access to nuclear weapons. For her part France refused to participate, not only on the grounds that the whole scheme was operationally unsound, but because Washington still insisted on the ultimate veto on the use of the nuclear weapon. The Johnson administration abandoned the scheme. France (and China) also refused to sign the Test Ban Treaty and attacked it as a blatant attempt by the Soviet Union and the United States to preserve their nuclear duopoly while denying other nations the opportunity to develop their own nuclear arsenals. Franco-American relations declined still further after 1962. During the Cuban missile crisis France supported the United States but de Gaulle resented the American failure to consult him prior to their quarantine decision. The French President bitterly attacked Johnson's handling of the Vietnam situation and in 1966 he withdrew France from military participation in NATO [9].

(viii) 1963 and after

The United States continued to hope that an arms limitation agreement with the Soviet Union would be possible after 1963. The launching of space satellites in 1960 permitted the United States to photograph sensitive parts of the Soviet Union from distances which made counter-measures impossible, and this seemed to obviate the need for any agreement on on-site inspection. McNamara had contemplated trying to minimise the risk to civilian populations in 1962 by developing the idea of 'city avoidance' strategy, whereby an American first strike would concentrate on destroying Soviet nuclear and armaments facilities, thus, he hoped, leaving open the possibility of negotiations before the United States launched its second salvo against Soviet cities. In 1964 McNamara abandoned this as too risky: nuclear attacks on Soviet missile sites would kill many Soviet citizens while the Soviet Union, with a much smaller arsenal, could not adopt a similar strategy and might, during a crisis, be tempted to launch a pre-emptive strike against the United States. After 1964 McNamara returned to the theory of 'city busting' or 'Mutual Assured Destruction' (MAD) as a safer means of deterring nuclear attack [46].

Kennedy's assassination in November 1963 in Dallas, Texas, left his successor, former Vice President Lyndon Johnson, with a large number of difficult and unresolved problems, not least the deteriorating situation in Vietnam which seemed to presage an imminent Vietcong victory. The world had changed significantly since the onset of the Cold War in the late 1940s. Decolonisation had resulted in the creation of a large number of new states whose instability presented fresh opportunities for Soviet and American intrigues and new dangers to world peace. The most serious of these events resulted from the sudden decision of Belgium to grant independence to the Congo on 30 June 1960, which was followed by a mutiny in its native army and a struggle for power by contending political factions which threatened to split the Congo apart. When the Soviet Union airlifted aid to the pro-Soviet faction, the United States threatened to intervene. A superpower confrontation was avoided when a United Nations force, masterminded by the Secretary General, Dag Hammarskjöld, and acting under General Assembly resolutions, landed in the Congo and attempted to restore order. By 1964 the United Nations had, after incredible confusion, imposed a semblance of order and the Soviet Union ceased to interefere in the country. However, Khrushchev loudly complained about Hammarskjöld's activities which, he claimed, had led to more bloodshed in the

Congo.

Indeed, the 1950s bi-polar division of the world was giving way to a more variegated system and the United States could no longer command automatic majorities in the General Assembly for her resolutions as she had been able to do in the 1950s. In a dramatic descent on the General Assembly in September 1960 Khrushchev demanded that the post of Secretary General be converted into a troika, with one secretary each to represent the interests of the West, the Soviet bloc and the Third World. This campaign was dropped after the death of Hammarskjöld in an aircrash in September 1961, but it demonstrated Soviet alarm over developments which might lead to the creation of a Third World bloc in the United Nations which might become as hostile to Soviet policies as was the West [49].

In October 1964 Khrushchev fell from power and was replaced as Secretary of the Communist Party by Leonid I. Brezhnev, a former Khrushchev aide. Khrushchev never fully recovered from the Cuban setback and by 1964 he had alienated practically all sections of the party hierarchy. His agricultural policies had been a disaster and the revival of his demands for cuts in the Red Army led the high command to campaign actively for his dismissal. Brezhnev inaugurated a more cautious Soviet policy. A first priority was to achieve Khrushchev's ambition of reaching parity with the USA in intercontinental ballistic missiles. McNamara did not respond by expanding the number of United States weapons systems, although the existing ones were made more deadly and accurate by the development of Multiple Independent Re-entry Vehicles. McNamara believed that a new arms race would be destabilising and out of all proportion to the advantages to be gained: for the same reason he opposed the deployment of an American anti-ballistic missile system. He believed that Soviet parity with the United States – he proposed a ceiling of about 1700 US land-based and sea-launched ICBMs – would ease the path of arms limitation talks. However, little progress was made during the 1960s, while the Soviet Union was building up her ICBM arsenal, and as a result of the increase in international tension following American air and ground intervention in Vietnam in 1965. *Détente* had to await the advent of Richard M. Nixon to the White House in 1969 and the end of direct American involvement in Vietnam in 1973.

(ix) Conclusion

In his farewell address as President on 17 January 1961 Eisenhower warned the American people that the Cold War had compelled the United States to create a permanent armaments industry of vast proportions and that 'in the councils of government, we must guard against the acquisition of unwarranted influence, whether sought or unsought, by the military-industrial complex. The potential for the disastrous rise of misplaced power exists and will persist' [6:*612*]. Eisenhower had, in the early years of his presidency, reduced military expenditure and, despite strong pressure from his military advisers and from Congress, had refused to increase it again after the shock of Sputnik. John F. Kennedy, however, reversed Eisenhower's defence policy and, despite concrete evidence that the so-called missile gap was 3:1 against the Soviet Union, insisted on increasing expenditure on missile research and development. He also expanded the size of American conventional forces and more money was spent on counter-insurgency and special forces such as the 'Green Berets'. The United States was thus provided with the military means to lend weight to Kennedy's 'New Frontier' concepts, and at the same time to feel secure from any Soviet threat. This tended to breed a feeling of over-confidence on the part of the administration which led, after Kennedy's death, to the United States becoming even more deeply embroiled in the Vietnam war. The costly failure of this war for the United States created a wave of disillusionment in the country which contributed to the retreat from the 'Imperial Presidency' in the 1970s.

General Conclusion

Before the First World War the great powers of Europe conformed to certain recognised standards of conduct which guided their policies and regulated their behaviour towards each other. Above all their diplomats, usually well-educated upper-class men, believed that it was possible to resolve differences between the powers by patient diplomacy and judicious compromises. When at times this proved to be impossible and crises became unmanageable, the so-called Concert of Europe would come into operation through the mechanism of conferences of the leading statesmen who would strive to reconcile their problems. While this Concert faltered after 1878, even as late as 1912 and 1913 a conference of ambassadors meeting in London under the British Foreign Secretary, Sir Edward Grey, successfully prevented the Balkan Wars from escalating into a major war between the great powers. The Concert however failed completely to function in 1914.

This shared assumption of a common interest in preserving peace was shattered by the First World War. The pre-1914 traditions were destroyed by the intense passions and hatreds generated by the war. The Bolshevik Revolution of 1917 in Russia produced a ferment of ideas which had nothing in common with the liberal traditions of Western Europe and the United States, and indeed was antagonistic towards them. The Bolsheviks believed that the struggle between capitalism and the proletariat could not be relaxed until communism had triumphed throughout the world. In this scenario communists did not distinguish between war and peace. Propaganda, internal subversion and conflict were essential weapons in the fight against capitalism. If there were compromises with the capitalist states these were merely tactical manoeuvres designed to persuade the capitalists to lower their guard while communism rallied its forces for a fresh onslaught. Western concepts of legality and constitutionalism had no place in Marxist-Leninist ideology, except in so far as they could be exploited for revolutionary purposes.

The post-1918 world was characterised by the clash of two competing ideologies. Both V.I. Lenin, the Soviet leader, and Woodrow Wilson, the American President, believed that they each possessed the sole prescription for a future peaceful world order. Wilson's concept of a world based on the principle of national self-determination and a League of Nations was repudiated by his own countrymen, but his ideas lived on until the Second World War when they became the basis for a renewed American effort to establish a stable post-war order. Communism survived in Russia after 1918 but did not succeed in extending its sway outside the Soviet Union until 1939.

The post-1914–18 war world also experienced the rise of fascism and national socialism in Italy and later in Germany. Born of the despair and disillusionment of the First World War, these *inter alia* drew on Social Darwinist and racist ideas which had been prevalent but not dominant in Europe before the war. National socialism also claimed to be anti-communist although its use of secret police and terroristic techniques was similar in many ways to those of the Soviet Union.

National socialism and communism in their different ways were perceived by the governing elites in Britain and France as threatening the very existence of their states, although national socialism appeared the greater menace since it was closer to hand. Europe was engulfed in war again in 1939, and this spread to the rest of the world in 1941. The victory of the 1941 Grand Coalition of the United States, Soviet Union and Britain over Germany, Italy and Japan seemed to pave the way for an era of peace and stability after the war, but these hopes were rudely shattered when the West interpreted Stalin's policy as expansionist and threatening. Soon the Soviet Union was perceived to be as evil as Hitler's

Germany had been.

As Britain continued to decline as an economic and military great power after 1945, the United States and the Soviet Union emerged as the only truly great powers. In 1914 there had been six European states who described themselves as great while, with the United States and Japan, there were five victor powers in 1918. The immense economic strength of the United States and the potential economic strength of the Soviet Union, together with their military and nuclear power after 1949, gave them the status of superpowers, towering above the rest of the world in power and influence.

These developments became more evident during the 1950s as the two superpowers competed with each other in developing more powerful nuclear delivery systems. Both sides appeared willing to go to the very 'brink' of war during crises. This was the decade when the East–West tensions of the so-called 'Cold War – a term which the veteran American journalist Walter Lippman coined in the mid-1940s – were at their height. In this highly tense situation efforts to end nuclear testing failed, despite the risks of fall-out and of accidents. Not until the late 1960s did a slightly more stable nuclear relationship become established. The Cuban missile crisis gave both superpowers a severe shock and led them to exercise more care in threatening each other with nuclear retaliation. However, it also encouraged the Soviet Union to accelerate her programme of nuclear research and development and by the early 1970s she had caught up with the United States in the number and quality of her delivery systems. Ironically this paved the way for limited strategic arms agreements and a measure of *détente* between them: the Soviet Union, now feeling more secure, felt she could afford to agree to a standstill in the deployment of certain categories of weapons. 'Mutual Assured Destruction' and 'second strike capabilities' also suggested a measure of caution and responsibility on the part of the leaders of the two powers.

Détente enjoyed only a short life. During the 1980s the United States, suspecting that the Soviet Union had used *détente* to steal a march on them in the development of shorter range and other nuclear missiles, embarked on a new rearmament programme. While the advent of new leaders in

97

the Kremlin has led to a renewed search for nuclear arms limitation the outcome is not yet a foregone conclusion. Relations between East and West remain tense, although the rivalry is much more muted in the mid-1980s than it was earlier in the decade. This has permitted an agreement on the limitation of theatre nuclear weapons in Europe: whether this will lead to further and more extensive agreements on missiles, and indeed to a renewed *détente*, is a matter for speculation.

Bibliography

[1]   Dean Acheson, *Present at the Creation: my Years in the State Department* (New York, 1969). An elegantly written account by Truman's last Secretary of State, who was the chief architect of containment.

[2]   G.M. Alexander, *The Prelude to the Truman Doctrine: British Policy in Greece 1944–1947* (Oxford, 1982). The Truman Doctrine was the first overt expression of American support for Western security. This book examines the background of Britain's intervention in the Greek civil war.

[3]   Richard A. Asiano, *American Defense Policy from Eisenhower to Kennedy: the Politics of Changing Military Requirements* (Ohio, 1975). A comprehensive account of the vicissitudes of American defence policy from Sputnik to the presidential election of John F. Kennedy.

[4]   Gar Alperovitz, *Atomic Diplomacy: Hiroshima and Potsdam* (New York, 1965). A 'New Left' historian who believes that the atomic bomb was intended as much to blackmail the Soviet Union into making concessions as to serve as an instrument to defeat Japan.

[5]   Stephen E. Ambrose, *Rise to Globalism: American Foreign Policy 1938–1970* (Baltimore, 1970). A useful textbook by one of the leading historians of the Cold War.

[6]   Stephen E. Ambrose, *Eisenhower: the President 1952–1969*, vol. II (London, 1984). An account of Eisenhower's internal and foreign policy based on his letters and papers. This is a sympathetic approach to the President's achievements.

[7]   Stephen E. Ambrose, *Nixon: 1913–1962* (New York, 1982). The first volume of a biography of Richard M. Nixon dealing with his earlier years as US Senator and Vice-President of the USA. It tries hard to be objective and to show that Nixon was not as black as he was painted by his contemporaries.

[8]   Terry H. Anderson, *The United States, Great Britain and the Cold War 1944–1947* (Missouri, 1981). A scholarly account of Anglo-American relations on the eve of the Cold War.

[9]   John Baylis, *Anglo-American Defence Relations 1939–1980: the*

Special Relationship (London, 1982). A short but judicious assessment of the 'special relationship' in defence matters.

[10] Charles E. Bohlen, *Witness to History 1929–1969* (New York, 1973). The memoirs of a senior American diplomat who played a leading role in many of the crises affecting the Soviet Union and the United States after 1945.

[11] Piers Brendon, *Ike: the Life and Times of Dwight D. Eisenhower* (London, 1987). A recent critical biography of Eisenhower.

[12] Symon Brown, *The Faces of Power: Constancy and Change in US Foreign Policy from Truman to Reagan* (Revised: New York, 1983).

[13] Alan Bullock, *Ernest Bevin: Foreign Secretary 1945–1951* (London, 1983). This excellent biography is essential reading if the Labour government's foreign policy is to be correctly understood. Bevin successfully gambled on an American commitment to European defence.

[14] Robert Dallek, *Franklin D. Roosevelt and American Foreign Policy 1932–1945* (New York, 1979). An outstanding favourable account of Roosevelt's foreign policy.

[15] A.W. De Porte, *Europe between the Superpowers: the Enduring Balance* (London, 1979). A stimulating analysis of the European States system and its post-1945 role between the Soviet Union and the United States.

[16] Robert A. Divine, *Roosevelt and World War II* (New York, 1969). A rather critical discussion of Roosevelt's handling of foreign affairs.

[17] Robert A. Divine, *Blowing on the Wind: the Nuclear Test Ban Debate 1954–1960* (New York, 1981). A sophisticated analysis of the long and unsuccessful discussions on a test ban treaty in the 1950s in the face of the increasing danger from nuclear fall-out.

[18] Robert A. Divine, *Eisenhower and the Cold War* (Oxford, 1981). The development of the Cold War in the 1950s.

[19] Herbert Feis, *From Trust to Terror: the Onset of the Cold War, 1945–46* (New York, 1957).

[20] Herbert Feis, *Between War and Peace: the Potsdam Conference* (Princeton, 1960).

[21] Herbert Feis, *Churchill, Roosevelt, Stalin: the War they Waged and the Peace they Sought* (Princeton, 1957). Although overtaken in many respects by subsequent research, these orthodox and standard accounts of the first years of the Cold War still contain useful information.

[22] Lawrence Freedman, *The Evolution of Nuclear Strategy* (London,

1982). Essential reading if the impact of nuclear weapons on strategic thinking and on superpower relations is to be fully understood.

[23] Edward Fursdon, *The European Defence Community: a History* (London, 1980). The standard account of this ultimately doomed effort to reconcile West German rearmament with French fears of a renewal of the German threat.

[24] John Lewis Gaddis, *The United States and the Origins of the Cold War 1941–1947* (New York, 1972). A fascinating account of how American opinion about the Soviet Union changed so dramatically during and after the Second World War.

[25] John Lewis Gaddis, *Strategies of Containment: a Critical Appraisal of Post War American Security Policy* (Oxford, 1982). A mature analysis of American national security policy to 1976 by a leading historian of the post-Vietnam school of American writers based on archival research and taking as its base George Kennan's influence on the containment debate.

[26] Norman A. Graebner, *Cold War Diplomacy: American Foreign Policy 1945–1975* (London, 1977). This interpretation of the Cold War, by one of the leading moderate revisionist writers, suggests that the root cause of America's dilemma in handling the Cold War has been her historic tendency to universalise her ideals which, after 1947, caused her to take on commitments worldwide which no nation, however strong, could for long sustain.

[27] Norman A. Graebner (ed.), *The National Security: its Theory and Practice 1945–1960* (Oxford, 1986). A useful collection of essays by younger American historians on how the Truman and Eisenhower administrations dealt with the pressures and problems of the Cold War.

[28] Albert Grosser, *The Western Alliance: European-American Relations since 1945* (London, 1980). A discussion of European perceptions of their relationship with the United States after the Second World War.

[29] Louis Hallé, *The Cold War as History* (New York, 1967). A revisionist critique of the origins of the Cold War, suggesting that the United States over-reacted to what were often defensive Soviet moves after 1945.

[30] Fraser J. Harbutt, *The Iron Curtain: Churchill, America and the Origins of the Cold War* (London, 1987). A detailed analysis of Churchill's role in converting American public opinion from a detached pro-Soviet view of international affairs to one of full-blown support for Britain and her overseas interests.

Interesting, but not entirely convincing.

[31] Max Hastings, *The Korean War* (London, 1987). The military aspects of the Korean War.

[32] Gregg Herken, *The Winning Weapon: the Atomic Bomb in the Cold War 1945–50* (New York, 1982).

[33] Townsend Hoopes, *The Devil and John Foster Dulles* (Boston, 1973). A hard hitting critique of the foreign policy of Dulles.

[34] Timothy P. Ireland, *Creating the Entangling Alliance: the Origins of NATO* (London, 1981). The United States hoped that her contribution to NATO would be psychological encouragement to the Europeans and that her military assistance would enable them to stand on their own feet and not depend too much on American troops.

[35] William K. Kaufmann, *The McNamara Strategy* (New York, 1971). A somewhat rosy and one-sided account of McNamara's policy as Secretary of Defense.

[36] George F. Kennan, *Memoirs 1925–1950* (Boston, 1967) and *Memoirs 1950–1963* (Boston, 1972). Kennan's role in United States diplomacy during the turbulent years after 1945 when relations with the Soviet Union reached their lowest ebb.

[37] Robert F. Kennedy, *Thirteen Years: a Memoir of the Cuban Missile Crisis* (New York, 1965). Robert Kennedy, President Kennedy's brother, was Attorney General during the Cuban Missile Crisis and this is his personal account of how it was handled.

[38] Henry A. Kissinger, *Nuclear Weapons and Foreign Policy* (New York, 1957). A contribution to the critique of Eisenhower's 'Massive Retaliation' Doctrine by the historian who subsequently became President Nixon's Secretary of State.

[39] Douglas Kinnard, *President Eisenhower and Strategy Management: a Study in Defense Politics* (Lexington, 1977).

[40] Joyce and Gabriel Kolko, *The Limits of Power: the World and United States Foreign Policy 1945–1954* (New York, 1972). A 'New Left' interpretation of the Cold War which blames American economic imperialism for the post-1945 events.

[41] B.R. Kuniholm, *The Origins of the Cold War in the Near East: Great Power Conflict in Iran, Turkey and Greece* (Princeton, 1980). Case studies of specific areas in the Near East in which the Cold War originated, based on research in American archives.

[42] Walter, La Feber, *America, Russia and the Cold War 1945–1980* (New York, 1980). A sound standard textbook.

[43] Carl A. Linden, *Khrushchev and the Soviet Leadership 1957–1964* (Maryland, 1966). An interesting account of Khrushchev's

internal and external struggles from Sputnik to his fall from power.

[44] Calum Macdonald, *Korea: the War before Vietnam* (London, 1986). A recent and balanced interpretation of the political and diplomatic background to the Korean War.

[45] Michael Mandelbaum, *The Nuclear Rvolution: International Politics before and after Hiroshima* (New York, 1981).

[46] Michael Mandelbaum, *The Nuclear Question: the United States and Nuclear Weapons* (New York, 1979). The impact of the atomic bomb on international relations and on American foreign policy during the Cold War.

[47] Vojech Mastny, *Russia's Road to the Cold War: Diplomacy, Warfare and the Politics of Communism 1941–45* (New York, 1979). Stalin's search for absolute security both inside and outside the Soviet Union inevitably resulted, the author claims, in a clash with the West after the Second World War.

[48] William McCagg, *Stalin Embattled: 1943–1948* (Detroit, 1978). Stalin was by no means all-powerful and secure towards the end of the Second World War, as contemporaries believed, and this book deals with his struggle to re-establish his absolute authority after 1943.

[49] Joseph L. Nogee and Robert H. Donaldson, *Soviet Foreign Policy since World War II* (Oxford, 1984). A general survey of Soviet foreign policy down to the 1980s.

[50] Yonusuke Nagai and Akira Iriye (eds), *The Origins of the Cold War in Asia* (New York, 1977). A useful collection of essays on the Asian dimension of the Cold War.

[51] Robert Osgood, *Limited War: the Challenge to American Strategy* (New York, 1957). One of the more perceptive critics of Eisenhower's 'Massive Retaliation' Doctrine.

[52] Robert Osgood, *NATO: the Entangling Alliance* (New York, 1962).

[53] Herbert S. Parmett, *JFK: the Presidency of John F. Kennedy* (London, 1984). A biography of the Kennedy years. To date there are no really satisfactory biographies of Kennedy, or comprehensive accounts of his policies.

[54] Thomas G. Paterson, *Postwar Reconstruction and the Origins of the Cold War* (London, 1973). The economic aspects of the Soviet-American confrontation after 1945.

[55] Victor Rothwell, *Britain and the Cold War 1941–1947* (London, 1982). This should really have been entitled 'The British Foreign Office and the Cold War' but it is none the worse for that.

103

[56] John Spanier, *American Foreign Policy since World War II* (2nd rev., New York, 1965).

[57] Strobe Talbott (trans. and ed.), *Khrushchev Remembers* (Boston, 1970). Suspected in the West at the time of publication of being a forgery, these memoirs are now generally accepted by historians as being authentic, although the testimony is one-sided and unreliable.

[58] William Taubman, *Stalin's American Policy: from Entente to Détente to Cold War* (New York, 1982).

[59] Adam B. Ulam, *The Rivals: America and Russia since World War II* (New York, 1975).

[60] Donald Cameron Watt, *Succeeding John Bull: America in Britain's Place 1900–1975* (Cambridge, 1984). A thought-provoking analysis of the causes and consequences of Britain's displacement by the United States as a world power.

[61] William Appleman Williams, *The Tragedy of American Diplomacy* (New York 1959). An elegantly written 'New Left' critique of American Cold War policy after 1945.

[62] Russell F. Weigley, *The American Way of War: History of United States Strategy and Military Policy* (New York, 1973). Part V of this history deals with the frustrations experienced by the American military in a post-war world where they have had to accept considerably less than total victory over an opponent.

[63] Daniel Yergin, *Shattered Peace: the Origins of the Cold War and the National Security State* (Boston, 1977). The US defence establishment's perceptions of the Soviet danger down to 1950, based on archival research in the USA.

Index

105

Dien Bien Phu, 64–5, 77, 88
Dulles, John Foster, 6, 61–4,
  67–8, 71–2, 77–8, 80

Eastern Europe, 14, 17, 19,
  22–4, 26–7, 30, 42–3, 50, 57,
  67, 71, 74
Eden, Anthony, 29, 68–70, 74
Egypt, 67–70
Eisenhower, Dwight D., 5–6, 56,
  60–4, 70–1, 73, 75–8, 80–1,
  83–4, 88, 94
Elbe River, 55
European Defence Community
  (EDC), 56, 74
European Recovery Act, 42–3,
  55, 58

Finland, 10, 12, 66
First World War, 8, 95–6
Formosa, 50–1, 54, 68, 72, 75
Forrestal, James F., 24
France, 10–13, 18–20, 22–3,
  36–7, 41, 43, 46, 52–5, 58,
  64–5, 68–71, 74, 89–91

Gaddis, John Lewis, 3
Geneva Conference (1954), 64–5
Germany, 10–14, 17–21, 25,
  27–30, 32, 36–7, 44–6, 53–7,
  74–5, 82–3, 87, 89–91, 96–7
Graebner, Norman, 4
Greece, 18, 23, 29, 40–1, 47–8
Grey, Sir Edward, 95
Guatemala, 82

Hammarskjöld, Dag, 92–3
Harriman, Averell W., 24, 26
Hiroshima, 27
Hitler, Adolf, 10–12, 96
Ho Chi Minh, 54, 64–5, 84
Holland, see the Netherlands
Hoover, Herbert, 60
Hopkins, Harry, 24–5
Hull, Cordell, 14
Hungary, 18, 29, 71–2

Iceland, 47
Inchon, 52

India, 11, 67–8, 75
Indochina, 53–5, 64–5, 77–9, 89
Iran, 37–8, 57, 68, 82
Iraq, 68–9, 71
Israel, 67, 69
Italy, 13, 18, 23, 28–30, 41, 43,
  47, 55–6, 74, 85, 96

Japan, 4, 9, 13–14, 21, 25–7,
  30–3, 50–2, 54, 68, 84, 96–7
Johnson, Lyndon B., 7, 73, 80,
  84, 91–2
Jordan, 69, 71

Kadar, Janos, 71
Kaganovitch, Lazar, 75
Kars, 28
Kennan, George F., 2, 10, 57
Kennedy, John F., 6, 60, 73, 79,
  80–9, 91–2, 94
Kennedy, Robert, 86
Khrushchev, Nikita, 4, 6, 66–7,
  70–2, 74–8, 80, 82–3, 85–7,
  92–3
Kim Il Sung, 51
Korea, 6, 50–4, 58, 60, 62, 65,
  68, 77, 79
Korean War, 47, 51–4, 58–60,
  62–3, 65, 77
Kuomintang, 48
Kurile Islands, 21

Laos, 83
League of Nations, 5, 8–9, 11,
  16, 18, 96
Leahy, Admiral William D., 24
Lebanon, 71
Lend lease, 13, 26, 37
Lenin, V. I., 5, 8–9, 11, 96
Liberated Europe, Declaration
  on, 22, 29
Libya, 30–1
Lippman, Walter, 97
London Conference of Foreign
  Ministers (1945), 28, 30–2
Luxembourg, 46, 56

MacArthur, General Douglas,
  32, 52–3, 59

Macmillan, Harold, 70–1, 91
Malenkov, Georgi M., 6, 31, 61–2, 66, 75
Manhattan Project, 26
Mao Tse-tung, 23, 50–2, 58, 62, 67, 75
Marshall, General George C., 24, 39, 41–3
Marshall Plan, *see* European Recovery Act
Marx, Karl, 5, 96
Matsu, 72, 77
McCarthy, Senator Joseph, 61
McMahon Act, 36
McNamara, Robert S., 80–1, 86, 90–3
Mediterranean, 31, 40, 57
Michael, King of Romania, 29
Middle East, 31, 34, 40, 46, 48, 67–71, 78–9
Molotov, V. M., 20, 24–5, 28, 30–2, 35, 42, 66, 75
Montreux Convention, 28, 30
Morganthau Plan, 20
Morocco, 89
Moscow Agreement (October 1944), 18, 23, 29
Moscow Conference of Foreign Ministers (1945), 32–4
Moscow Conference of Foreign Ministers (1947), 41
Multilateral Fleet (MLF), 91
Mussaddiq, Muhammad, 82
Mussolini, Benito, 28
Mutual Assured Destruction (MAD), 92, 97

Nagasaki, 27
Nagy, Imry, 71
Nasser, Colonel Abdul Gamel, 68–70
National Security Council (NSC), 49, 53
Nazi-Soviet Pact (1939), 10, 12, 14
Netherlands, the, 44, 46, 56
New Look, the, 62–4
New Zealand, 68
Nixon, Richard M., 7, 79, 94

North Atlantic Treaty Organisation (NATO), 44, 47, 53–5, 58, 63, 74, 90–1
Norway, 47

Oder-Neisse Line, 17, 21, 27
Okinawa, 50, 54

Pakistan, 68
Palestine, 36
Paris Economic Conference (1947), 42
Paris Peace Conference (1919), 8–9, 11
Pearl Harbor, 13
'Percentages' Agreement (October 1944), *see* Moscow Agreement (October 1944)
Philippines, the, 31, 50, 68
Pigs, Bay of, 82–3
Pleven Plan, *see* European Defence Community
Poland, 10, 12, 17, 21, 23–5, 27, 58, 71
Polaris, 81, 90–1
Portugal, 47
Potsdam Conference, 27–30

Quemoy, 72, 77

Radford, Admiral Arthur W., 64
Reagan, Ronald, 7
Rhee, Syngman, 51–2
Rhine River, 54
Ridgway, General Matthew, 64
Romania, 18, 28–9, 32–3
Roosevelt, Franklin Delano, 9, 12–25, 36
Ruhr, the, 37, 55
Rusk, Dean, 86

Sakhalin Island, 21
San Francisco Conference (1945), 20, 24
Saudi Arabia, 69
Schuman Plan, 55
Second Front, 13
Second World War, 2–3, 10, 12–23, 35, 96

107

Skybolt, 90–1
South East Asia Treaty
  Organisation (SEATO), 68
Sputnik I, 72
Stalin, Joseph V., 2–4, 9–10,
  13–14, 17–29, 32–5, 38, 40,
  42–4, 46, 50–1, 53, 56–8, 61,
  66–7, 71, 74, 78, 96
State Department, 10, 24, 38,
  42, 49, 57, 87
Stimson, Henry L., 24, 26, 38
Strachey, John, 29
Straits, the *see* Dardanelles
Suez Canal, 68–70
Suez Crisis (1956), 68–72,
  89–90
Supreme Headquarters, Allied
  Powers in Europe (SHAPE),
  56
Syria, 69–70

Taiwan, *see* Formosa
Teheran Conference (1943), 17,
  19, 21
Test Ban Treaty (1963), 88–9,
  91
Thailand, 68
Tito, Marshall, 23–5, 29, 40,
  43, 50, 66
Trieste, 29, 35
Truman, Harry S., 5, 12, 23–7,
  29, 31, 33–5, 38–40, 45–6,

48–50, 52–60, 68, 78, 88
Tunisia, 89
Turkey, 28, 31, 40, 47, 68, 78,
  85, 87

United Arab Republic, 70–1
United Kingdom, *see* Britain
United Nations, 16, 18, 20, 22,
  38, 52–3, 60, 70, 72, 76, 85,
  92–3

Vandenberg, Senator Arthur H.,
  47
Vietcong, 84, 92
Vietnam, 2, 5–7, 65, 79, 83–4,
  91–4
Vyshinsky, Andrei, 28–9

Wallace, Henry A., 39
Warsaw Pact, 74
Western European Union (WEU),
  see Brussels Pact
Wilson, Woodrow, 5, 8, 16, 96

Yalta Conference (1945), 17,
  19–25, 28, 30
Yalu River, 52
Yemen, the, 69
Yugoslavia, 18, 22–3, 29, 40,
  43, 50, 74

Zhadanov, 32, 43